Many of us have experienced being in a situation where another language is being spoken. This can be an exciting adventure, but also hard work! Through his book, Jonathan leads us to reflect on the importance of languages used in church. He encourages us to see that a vision for a multilingual church is founded in biblical principles. He recognizes the challenges this presents and takes his reader on a journey through different options a church might use, the pros and cons, and questions to reflect on. Jonathan writes in an engaging and accessible way, helping us to see how we might ensure our churches reflect our local communities in the fullest sense, in a way that honors God and all his people.

EMMA BILLINGTON
Head of National Development, Welcome Churches

Have you ever dreamed of being part of an intercultural church where everyone feels welcomed, needed and known? If so, then you'll have found yourself wondering how can we be a healthy church family when we speak different languages? In Multilingual Church, Jonathan Downie doesn't sugar-coat the challenges, but, as an expert guide, he shows the paths you could follow and warns of the potential pitfalls. More than that, he presents a compelling, biblically grounded vision of how multilingual churches are a powerful witness to the power of the Gospel in our divided and diverse communities. I heartily commend this much needed book!

ADAM MARTIN
National Director, Intercultural Churches UK

Jonathan Downie has written an honest easy-to-read guide for churches and Christian communities who desire to become a place of belonging, where people of all backgrounds feel welcome. Jonathan acknowledges that every church has different challenges to becoming multilingual and rather than being prescriptive, he provides research-based tools and suggestions. I appreciate that Jonathan's approach is not just to church leadership but to individuals wanting to apply this approach in their everyday life.

While this book is about the power of being welcome and belonging, it also presents a challenge and an invitation. I appreciate Jonathan's anecdotal writing style backed by serious research. You will be able to read it swiftly, but the questions it raises will linger. Are we willing to be those who truly serve those who we say we want to reach? After reading this book you'll be ready to roll up your proverbial sleeves and respond "yes" as you think through how to make the church look more like our multiethnic communities and most importantly like Heaven!

REV. TERESA PARISH, PHD
Founder KITE Ministries

At Pentecost, we're told the people heard about the mighty power of the Holy Spirit in their native language. In Revelation, every tribe and language will stand before the Lamb. It's here, in the in between, Jonathan Downie speaks a prophetic word to the Church—a calling to create spaces where a diverse group can gather together as a multicultural tapestry and find our full identity in Christ. We're at a unique time in history to do this, and do it well.

TRACI RHOADES
Author, *Shaky Ground: What to Do After the Bottom Drops Out*

Multilingual Church by Jonathan Downie is an answer to prayer! It is a well-founded theological and biblical workbook for all of us serving in multicultural, multilingual contexts. As Jonathan so eloquently explains in this book, a multilingual church is more than a strategy to reach other people, it is a revelation, a vision from God.

If the ultimate goal is to bring every nation, culture, and language in unity in front of the eternal throne of grace, shouldn't we make every effort today to bring multiple cultures and languages together to worship God? Downie's book answers this question by affirming that multicultural church necessarily needs to reflect the multilingual reality of its people. The clear vision, thorough analysis, and clear step-by-step approach Jonathan adopts in this book are a great help for every pastor and church leadership team who wants to become an inclusive multilingual church. Furthermore this book is a great tool for church planters in North America and Europe where a diversity of languages and cultures are intermingling in our cities and nations. As the Lead Pastor of a multilingual church in America, I encourage my fellow co-workers in the kingdom to read and take to heart the vision presented in this book. After all, we are called as the church of the living Christ to celebrate, include and bring to the table in a dignified manner every culture and language represented in our context.

FIKRI YOUSSEF, DMIN
Senior Pastor, La Casa Church, Nashville, TN

MULTILINGUAL CHURCH

Strategies for Making Disciples in All Languages

JONATHAN DOWNIE

Multilingual Church: Strategies for Making Disciples in All Languages

© 2024 by Jonathan Downie. All Rights Reserved.

No part of this book may be reproduced, stored in a retrieval system, or transmitted in any form or by any means—electronic, mechanical, photocopy, recording, or otherwise—without prior written permission from the publisher, except brief quotations used in connection with reviews. For permission, email permissions@wclbooks.com. For corrections, email editor@wclbooks.com.

William Carey Publishing (WCP) publishes resources to shape and advance the missiological conversation in the world. We publish a broad range of thought-provoking books and do not necessarily endorse all opinions set forth here or in works referenced within this book. WCP can't verify the accuracy of website URLs beyond the date of print publication.

Scripture quotations marked NRSV are taken from the New Revised Standard Version Bible, copyright © 1989 National Council of the Churches of Christ in the United States of America. Used by permission. All rights reserved worldwide.

Scripture quotations marked NLT are taken from the Holy Bible, New Living Translation, copyright ©1996, 2004, 2015 by Tyndale House Foundation. Used by permission of Tyndale House Publishers, Carol Stream, Illinois 60188. All rights reserved.

Scripture quotations marked NASB are taken from the NASB® New American Bible®, Copyright © 1960, 1971, 1977, 1995, 2020 by The Lockman Foundation. Used by permission. All rights reserved. lockman.org.

Scripture quotations marked NIV are taken from the Holy Bible, New International Version®, NIV®. Copyright © 1973, 1978, 1984, 2011 by Biblica, Inc.™ Used by permission of Zondervan. All rights reserved worldwide. www.zondervan.com. The "NIV" and "New International Version" are trademarks registered in the United States Patent and Trademark Office by Biblica, Inc.™

Scripture quotations marked MSG are taken from THE MESSAGE, copyright © 1993, 2002, 2018 by Eugene H. Peterson. Used by permission of NavPress, represented by Tyndale House Publishers. All rights reserved.

Published by William Carey Publishing
10 W. Dry Creek Cir
Littleton, CO 80120 | www.missionbooks.org

William Carey Publishing is a ministry of Frontier Ventures
Pasadena, CA | www.frontierventures.org

Cover and Interior Designer: Mike Riester

ISBNs: 978-1-64508-536-2 (paperback)
        978-1-64508-538-6 (epub)

Printed Worldwide

28 27 26 25 24   1 2 3 4 5   IN

Library of Congress Control Number: 2024930154

DEDICATION

This book is dedicated to every single church leader who is doing their best to reach, teach, and disciple their multilingual communities. We do this solely for the glory of God and for the advancement of the kingdom. As you proclaim the gospel of Jesus's death, resurrection, and reign, may you see this gospel change your community forever.

It is also dedicated to my wife, Helen, who has believed in me even when I was on the verge of giving up, who has stood by me through trials, and who sets a wonderful example every day of how to be a godly wife and mother.

CONTENTS

Foreword by Dr. Harvey Kwiyani — ix
Introduction: When Church Can Reach Everyone — xiii

Part I: The Basics

Chapter 1: Why Multilingual Church Matters — 3
Chapter 2: Multilingual Church Is Biblical — 13

Part II: Common Ways to Do Multilingual Church

Chapter 3: They'll All Learn Our Language Anyway — 31
Chapter 4: Add Services in Difference Languages? — 37
Chapter 5: Different Languages, One Service — 45
Chapter 6: Artificial Intelligence to the Rescue? — 55
Chapter 7: Interpreting in the Corner — 63
Chapter 8: We Have a Vision for Languages—One Day We'll Need Them — 73
Chapter 9: Languages Are Who We Are — 79

Part III: Vision, Strategy, and Implementation

Chapter 10: A Vision for Languages — 89
Chapter 11: Strategy—The When and Where — 97
Chapter 12: Implementation—The Who and How — 105
Chapter 13: Maintenance—The Future — 129

Part IV: Sunday Is Just the Start

Chapter 14: Excluding the Locals? — 137
Chapter 15: Sunday Is Just the Start — 143
Chapter 16: Getting Help — 149

Afterword by Pastor Mike Lemay — **153**
Acknowledgments — **155**
Bibliography — **157**

FOREWORD

The body of Christ around the world is inherently multilingual. Today, in the early decades of the twenty-first century, as Christianity continues to explode in large parts of this shrinking global village, all major languages are represented in the Christian community. Spanish continues to be the language spoken by most Christians in the world today. After it comes a plethora of other languages used to glorify the name of Christ by Christians in different parts of the world: English, Mandarin, Cantonese, Yoruba, Portuguese, Xhosa, etc. Of course, the list is long and includes all major languages in the world, from Afrikaans to Zulu. As Christianity grows in the non-Western world, the significance of Majority World languages within the Christian community increases. For instance, more Christians speak Yoruba than German. Furthermore, there are more Luganda-speaking Anglicans in Uganda than English-speaking ones in England. This shift will have implications for all of us. As such, we need to begin to pay attention to the role of languages in our theology, missiology, and ecclesiology.

In this sense, I find Jonathan Downie's argument in this book groundbreaking, especially here in the West (more so in Europe than in America, to be fair), where there is almost always one dominant language against which all other languages are measured: English for the United Kingdom and Ireland, French for France, Italian for Italy, and many others. If a person is unable to converse in these main languages, they will inevitably be left out. Life can move on without them. Thus, languages often determine who is in and who is out of a society. Further, languages have been used to colonize people. In his book, *Decolonising the Mind*, Ngugi wa Thiong'o eloquently argues that languages are the most effective tools in the colonial process.

Of course, it is no secret languages have power. We often use languages—English, German, Italian, or any other language for that matter—to include, exclude, or dominate people. Those who can speak some languages are more welcome than those who cannot. In some parts of Europe where various dialects are prevalent, it is not enough to speak a language—people must get the dialect right as well. Among migrants who have come to Europe from other parts of the world, they have not only to learn the language of the country they have migrated to, they must also master their accents as well in order to be more welcome. Being on the wrong side of linguistic barriers can mean being left behind in many areas of life. In this context Jonathan reminds us that our worship must be hospitable to all nations, tribes, and tongues. Multilingual worship services say to those who are linguistic outsiders that they are seen and welcome. It is Hospitality 101.

In this era of world Christianity, when we gather as a global fellowship of followers of Christ, included among us are people from almost all nations, tribes, and languages. We embody that powerful image of Revelation 9 where multitudes from the nations worship before the throne. Some of us in the West can actually experience a small portion of that global fellowship in our own cities. Christians from around the world worship Christ in their languages in London, Manchester, Glasgow, and many other Western cities. In Liverpool, where I am located, I know Ghanaian churches who worship in Twi. I also know Nigerian churches that worship in Yoruba, Ethiopian churches that worship in Amharic, Zimbabwean churches that worship in Shona, Chinese churches that worship in Mandarin or Cantonese, Brazilian churches that worship in Portuguese, plus many others. Without a doubt, the languages of the nations are here. Thus, Christian communities in our cities are already multilingual. The underlying question of this book is, "what would it take for congregations to become multilingual?" It would be a great blessing to our cities if these diverse Christian communities found a way to unite in their worship, and, as Jonathan shows us in this book, language should not be the barrier that makes this impossible in the twenty-first century.

Jonathan's argument in this book is perfectly clear. You do not need to wrestle rigorously with it to understand what he is saying—Christian congregations must attend to languages spoken among their members (and guests) in order to be faithful to their context and to stay relevant and hospitable in a world of exclusion and division.

In a nutshell, congregations located in multicultural contexts need to consider having more than one language spoken (and heard) in their worship services. Doing so honors God who shows no favoritism (Acts 10:34) and is no respecter of persons (Rom 2:11). It also dignifies those among us who find themselves worshipping with people speaking languages other than their own. It is a strong kenotic gesture to allow ourselves to attend to others linguistic needs.

Painstakingly, Jonathan walks us through the Scriptures to show us how attention to multilingualism is not only something we find in the Bible but also God's idea for the church. Indeed, he takes us through parts of the Gospels and Acts to show how God not only expands the church but is keen to include the linguistic other. The shift from Jerusalem to

Antioch and beyond is not only geographical or societal, but also linguistic. *Jehoshua* became *Iesous* and the *Messiah* would become the *Lord*. As God has expanded the story of the church, God also welcomed new languages into the fellowship of the Spirit. This story is still going on today. God is still drawing nations, tribes, and tongues (otherwise translated as "languages") into the kingdom; this unfolding will continue until all have heard the gospel and are represented in the famous crowd beneath the throne (Rev 9). With this in mind, churches ought to behave in accordance with the fact that God's kingdom is a domain of many languages.

This call for multilingual churches is necessary, especially now when the global village is shrinking rapidly. Current migration trends mean that the nations—with their languages—are mixing all over the world in ways that have not been possible before. Here in the UK, it is possible to meet people from almost every country in the world. The same can be said of many Western countries. Some migrants are Christians but many of them have yet to hear the gospel in a meaningful way.

Additionally, the internet makes it possible for people to fellowship with others from different parts of the world. Jonathan eloquently explains how the COVID-19 pandemic changed a great deal of how we participate in church. Multilingual churches are not only for local churches in contexts whose demographics are changing. They also serve the global fellowship of believers who want to be enriched by God's gifts given to another community elsewhere. I know many Malawian Christians, for example, who follow Western sermon podcasts religiously because they are in English. Yet, I also know many Malawian preachers who, given an opportunity and good interpretation, could be a blessing to Christians in the West. This is where multilingual churches have the potential to bring the parts of the body of Christ closer together.

For many of us who have come from Africa, Asia, or Latin America, our communities and, therefore, our churches are often multilingual. In the immediate community where I grew up in Malawi, almost everyone was multilingual. I grew up speaking four languages, including English which we learned in school. I would later learn French and German. My mother spoke Chichewa, Chiyao, and Chishona (she was born and bred in Zimbabwe). My father spoke Chichewa and Chilomwe and could understand Chiyao. Many people in my area spoke at least two or three of the five common languages.

One key practice that was foundational to our communal life was to switch languages depending on who we were talking to. Whenever we met with others, be it at school, at work, or at church, it was normal to incorporate several languages in one conversation. It was almost natural to seek to determine what language others were most comfortable in so that we could make them feel welcome. Even in church—rather, *especially* in church—our multilingualism was of great use. Our services reflected the multilingual community in which we were located. We could read a Chichewa Bible, sing Chiyao and Chilomwe songs, and have the sermon preached in English (which generally served as the lingua franca), often with translation. In doing so, every language present was included in the service.

Jonathan's vision of multilingual churches offers more to our Christian communities than a solution to our linguistic division. It proposes a way for us to be more united with our brothers and sisters who are of a different linguistic tribe. It also shows us a way to be hospitable to one another, especially to migrants and strangers who speak different languages from our own. It is my prayer that as you read this book, a fire will burn in your heart for the nations (who speak different languages from your own), both overseas and in your neighborhood.

HARVEY KWIYANI, PHD
Liverpool, 2024

INTRODUCTION

When Church Can Reach Everyone

I was only in Germany to visit my girlfriend. I did not expect a date with my calling. Yet here I was, in Germany for the second time, experiencing interpreting for the second time, and being reminded why I had become so excited about it in the first place. Right there, I saw what a multilingual church could look like, and I knew I was called to give my life to see this happen again and again around the world.

I had decided to train as an interpreter a couple of years earlier, after seeing interpreting at a Christian youth conference in Germany. But I had never actually seen interpreting equipment, since the first interpreters I saw had worked on stage, alongside the preacher. Yet, as soon as you walked into the sanctuary of this church, there was a smiling face, asking in German and English which language you needed and offering you a small, clip-on receiver. A quick turn of the receiver dial to channel one got you English. Channel two got you French. Channel three was for Chinese and so on. All these languages provided by interpreters perched in small cubicles on the balcony above my head.

Here I was, not knowing enough German to catch a train, but able to participate fully and wholeheartedly in a service in a German church. The interpreting was not the only part of the picture, though. The sung worship was in two or three or more languages. There were house groups in different languages and people obviously felt comfortable coming to church in clothes that represented their culture. For me, this was a little slice of heaven.

A couple of years after that visit, I married that girlfriend. I didn't know then that my career over the next two decades would land me in larger versions of those booths, or have me delivering interpreting from home, or talking and researching about interpreting. What I did know was that churches like that one in Germany were the kinds of places I wanted to be in.

I revisited that church a few more times and got to know the leaders. Pastor Mario Wahnschaffe's book on the church, entitled *Building an International Church*, gives a flavor of the challenges of building and sustaining a church like his. It is a book we will return to later. I am continually struck by the importance of these multilingual churches.

The Challenge of Multilingual Communities

Walk through the center of any modern city and you will hear several languages being spoken. Walk into many modern workplaces and you will meet people who work in a different country than the one in which they were born.

Yet walk into most churches in Europe and North America and you will hear a single language through the service and most likely only see people with a single skin color. The world around us is multicultural, multilingual, and diverse. Our churches often aren't. Sadly, sometimes even when churches try to reflect the diversity around them, their efforts lead nowhere.

The wider issue of multiethnic church has occupied theologians and sociologists for some time now. Books by Mark DeYmaz, Derwin Gray, and Korie Little Edwards, among others, have made the case for multiethnic church and mapped out the attitudes and leadership approaches needed to sustain them. Such work is incredibly valuable and important. What often gets overlooked, however, is that to reach our multicultural communities, churches need to take on the challenge of dealing with linguistic differences.

Consider the church in the west of Scotland I attended in my teens and twenties. The church was in a small, ex-industrial town called Wishaw. The vast majority of the people there were Scots. From the moment the church was planted, the pressing issue seemed to be reaching people in the struggling, underfunded council housing estates that surrounded the buildings where we met. Becoming multilingual was not on the agenda when there were so many immediate, pressing needs. Before it folded, the church would end up running a charity shop and a shop for collecting and reselling furniture, both of which helped to preach the gospel by providing employment opportunities and showing love to the people in the town.

> *The world around us is multicultural, multilingual, and diverse. Our churches often aren't.*

One day, some people from the Democratic Republic of Congo arrived. They knew no English and only one person in the congregation knew how to interpret into French (me!). When they attended, the church suddenly became multiethnic. Becoming multiethnic required the church to become multilingual. In that case, a multiethnic church could not be separated from multilingual church.

For that small church in Scotland, becoming multilingual became too much. Within a few months of arriving, the visitors left and were never seen again. The issue of linguistic difference could not be solved by having one person in the church who spoke the language and hoping that would be enough. Linguistic difference was just an echo of wider cultural differences and the challenge of people being able to understand the service was a microcosm of the challenge of building a church that could really reach and disciple everyone in the community.

In other places around the world, becoming multilingual might not require the church to become multiethnic at all. In countries like Canada, not being multilingual means excluding a large part of the population. In parts of Africa and Asia, monolingual churches simply don't make sense when people might speak one language at work and another at home. There, the language choices churches make end up being powerful political and theological statements about the church and its attitudes to the people around it. In fact, the languages used by churches in multicultural cities always make those statements. We just might not always be aware of it.

What Is Multilingual Church, Anyway?

When we think about multilingual church, it isn't enough to just imagine a church where a few people can converse in another language. While parts of this book will be dedicated to the tricky details of ensuring that people can hear or see your church services in the language they speak or sign, that is just the start. A church that can reach, teach, and disciple everyone in a community isn't just a church where people speak different languages, but a church where people of all cultural and language backgrounds are welcome. How we serve people who have different language needs is important. How our service percolates into the way we think about church, lead the church, and plan church life is even more important.

This book is for every church looking to reach, teach, and disciple people from every background: from the bustling city church that offers interpreting every week and has home groups in a range of languages, to the small church struggling to make people from another country feel at home. This book will explain why multilingual church matters, considering both the demographic realities of modern cities and repeated Biblical precedent. It will also explain the different ways that churches can meet the language needs of their congregations and communities.

At this point, I probably need to insert a few quick definitions, since I know that not everyone reading this book will be familiar with the different kinds of language provision available. For a start, in this book "language provision" and occasionally "language services" will be used as catch-all terms for anything churches can do to meet people's language needs. This covers everything from making written materials available in a particular language, to having church services in different languages, using apps, and various kinds of translation and interpreting. If it allows people to understand in their language, it's part of language provision and language services. Those terms need to be wide because the range of solutions available to churches is wide.

Within that vast range, I know most about two specific ways of offering language provision. The first is translation. Translation in this book will refer exclusively to the production of a fixed, written, subtitled, or sign language text on the basis of another fixed text. Usually, we think of translation as going from one written language to another, for example Bible translations, translations of novels, and more importantly for this book, the translation of liturgies, orders of services, songs, church bulletins and similar texts.

Since new technologies have hugely multiplied the kinds of translations available and the languages they can appear in, one way to remember what translation is here is that translation always happens when the original text is already finished. Once the liturgy is written, the video is edited, the bulletin is finalized, or the song is complete in its original language, translators come along and create a new version in another language.

Translation differs from interpreting, which in this book will refer to the creation of a spoken or sign language version of what was said or signed, while the event is still going on. Interpreting can happen when someone does a short prayer at a church dinner and the interpreter waits until they have finished praying before giving a version in another language. It could mean people in soundproof booths or remote studios providing simultaneous interpreting of the service while it is happening. It could even mean someone in a home group interpreting someone's story sentence-by-sentence as they tell it. Interpreting is there in the moment, at the service, at the meeting, in the event, alongside the speakers or signers.

Within translation and interpreting, and certainly within language provision as a whole, there is an almost inexhaustible variety of approaches, methods, strategies and techniques churches can use. In this book, we will cover some of the most common and most researched, especially since many options are essentially variations of the ones covered here.

Introduction | xvii

There are no one-size-fits-all solutions. One church might be happy to use remote interpreting technology to pull in professional interpreters from around the world, while providing home groups in several languages. Another might find it useful to start a dedicated Sunday service for a specific language group. Still another could decide to have an interpreter from the church on stage with the preacher. There are many possible choices and each one has its own benefits and challenges.

What is often missed is that sustaining any kind of language provision and making it a success requires more than just setting something up and hoping it works. Based on research from real churches and other interpreting organizations, we will explore the factors that help make it possible to keep reaching, teaching, and discipling people who speak different languages, even once the initial excitement and passion has worn off. Finally, we will provide an honest account of what happens to a church when it becomes multilingual and how that affects all aspects of church life, from preaching to leadership.

> **There are no one-size-fits-all solutions.**

The Structure of This Book

In part one, we will look at the demographic and theological reasons why multilingual church is not just a good idea but a God idea. Part two covers the most common approaches that churches use. In this part, I deliberately tell the story of these options in terms of how people will experience them and the messages they send before anyone even speaks a word. I have also treated them independently, even though, as I will argue later, they often work best in combination.

Part three walks through the four steps of multilingual church. These are vision, strategy, implementation, and maintenance. This section pulls together the knowledge from previous parts and turns it into practical applications for any church. I make no apologies for these sections having more questions than answers. My aim is not to tell a church how to do multilingual church but to hand over as many tools as possible to empower you to walk through that journey.

Part four concludes the book by exploring how all this can work out in the everyday life of the church, even away from Sunday services. It also includes a short chapter of resources for further help.

It is often tempting to think of multilingual church as something that might happen by accident or as something that will take care of itself. While it would be nice if that were true, this book describes the journey of discovering the challenges and rewards of building a multilingual church. We cannot deny that the challenges are great, but the rewards are nothing less than a representation of heaven on earth. Before we get there, however, we need to understand just how big the need is.

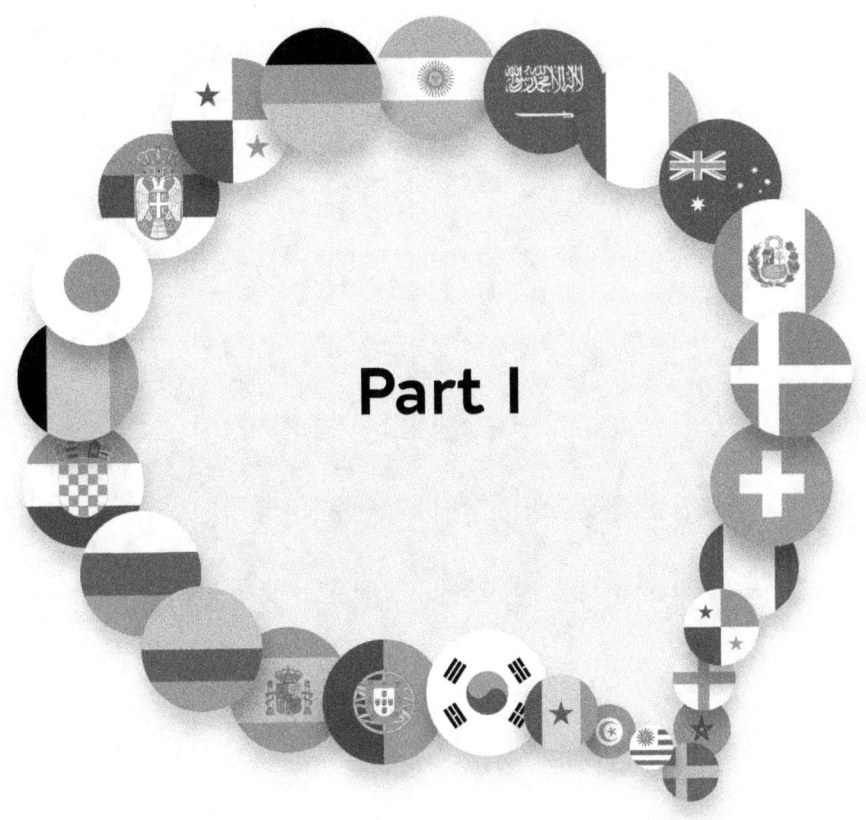

Part I

The Basics

CHAPTER 1

Why Multilingual Church Matters

If we want to know why churches should consider becoming multilingual, we can start with one simple fact. Every modern city is multilingual.

One of the barbers in town moved here from Poland. My sister-in-law is from the Philippines. One of my Romanian colleagues recently gave birth in a hospital in Glasgow. Even in smaller towns in the UK, it is normal to meet people who have moved from South Africa, the US, or Ukraine. This pattern repeats across Europe and much of the world.

Every modern city is multilingual, but how many churches are? Why does that even matter? Let's start with a very simple example.

A Personal Example of Why Multilingual Church Matters

While working abroad as part of my undergraduate degree, I spent an academic year in Dunkirk, in the far north of France. This was challenging enough for me, with three years of undergraduate-level French classes under my belt. It was much more challenging for my girlfriend, now my wife, when she visited. She had almost no French and stayed with an older lady in the church who had almost no English.

Church services were held in French only, with me offering a bit of whispered interpreting. (We will talk more about that kind of interpreting in chapters 7 and 12.) While she might have known the tunes of some songs, the words were completely meaningless. If I tired during the service, she lost the ability to participate. If I had to deal gently with someone asking me to be quiet, she missed what was being said.

> *Every modern city is multilingual, but how many churches are?*

True, she was one person without French in an overwhelmingly French-speaking church, but her experience is repeated over and over again by refugees, students, visiting workers, those fleeing persecution, travelers, and holidaymakers. Imagine fleeing war, persecution, or poverty, only to find yourself in a strange church in a strange country where you have no idea what is happening. How powerful would it be to hear or see your language being spoken or signed?

Contrast my wife's experience in France with the one we had when visiting a church in Vienna, Austria. I was due to speak at an academic conference and, since I don't leave home for more than a couple of nights without my family, we extended our stay to make it a family holiday. Since my wife speaks fluent German, the situation was even better.

While my wife speaks German, I do not. For the moment, my German just about extends to ordering a hot chocolate. We were pleased to find that Vienna has a church that styled itself as an "international church." I was even more pleased to find that, not only did the church sing worship in German and English (more on that approach in chapters 5, 11, and 12), but interpreting was provided during the entire sermon. My wife could enjoy the sermon in German while I heard English from the interpreter, who did an excellent job.

After the service, we attended a church meal where people happily spoke to us in English. One little decision—to make the service bilingual—made a big difference. Having people who spoke my language in the church made me feel that I belonged and could get to know people. Never mind that we were only there on holiday; we felt like people were genuinely happy that we were there.

Which kind of church is yours? Is yours the church that goes on in one language and isn't yet ready to welcome people who speak different ones? Is yours the church that welcomes people in diverse languages?

Notice that I asked if your church was the one that isn't *yet* ready to welcome people in different languages. I know from my own experience that the church in France was full of caring, warm, friendly, and approachable people. It is there that I had my first experience of interpreting for an entire conference. I owe a lot to that church. But when my wife visited, the church wasn't yet set up to welcome people who didn't speak French. With time and growth in capacity, any church can get there. But why should they even consider it?

Some Basic Facts and Figures

Stories like these are playing out in communities across the world right now. The reasons why people move countries are as varied as the people themselves, but the need to think seriously about multilingual church is surprisingly consistent. People arrive in a new place looking for a welcome and a way to fit in.

England and Wales are a case in point. According to the 2021 census, one in every six people living there was born outside the country.[1] A full 8.9 percent of the population of England and Wales does not use English (and/or Welsh in Wales) as their primary language.[2] In London alone, three

---

1 Office of National Statistics, "Transcript of Census 2021."
2 Office of National Statistics, "People, Population, and Community."

hundred different languages are spoken. Even outside of the largest cities, there are towns like Gateshead in the north of England, with a population of just under two hundred thousand, where ninety languages are spoken by school pupils and 7 percent of those pupils do not use English at home.[3]

In some cases, these people have arrived from countries where the gospel cannot be preached openly or where Christians are persecuted. For example, while Somalia is the second most dangerous country in the world to be a Christian,[4] 110,000 Somalis live in the UK.[5]

Of course, not all language differences are due to migration. My home country of Scotland has three national languages. Besides the 92.6 percent of the population who use English, there are 57,000 speakers of Gaelic and 13,000 users of British Sign Language.[6]

That pattern repeats across the world. In Chicago an estimated 30 percent of the population speak a language other than English at home.[7] In Perth, Australia, that figure is over 37 percent.[8]

You can find similar figures for France, the United States, Germany, and many other countries. Wherever you live, there will be a growing population of people who do not use your national languages or, what I will now call, the "locally dominant language" at home. This becomes even more complex in officially bilingual or multilingual countries such as Canada, Switzerland, or South Africa where the "locally dominant language" can and does change from area to area within the same country.

There will also be a significant population of people who, for whatever reason, do not use any of the locally dominant languages at all. If churches only present the gospel in a single language, those people cannot hear it. As the Bible reminds us:

> But how can they call on him to save them unless they believe in him? And how can they believe in him if they have never heard about him? And how can they hear about him unless someone tells them? (Rom 10:14, NLT)

Elsewhere, in a debate about the use of tongues in church, Paul points out an obvious fact that should resonate with churches today.

---

3 Glickman, "January 2018 School Census."
4 Open Doors, "World Watch List 2023."
5 Connor and Krogstad, "5 Facts."
6 National Records of Scotland, "Scotland's Census."
7 Riggio, "Map: The Languages."
8 City of Perth, "Languages Spoken at Home."

> There are many different languages in the world, and every language has meaning. But if I don't understand a language, I will be a foreigner to someone who speaks it, and the one who speaks it will be a foreigner to me. (1 Cor 14:10–11, NLT)

Whatever one's theological view about the meaning of "tongues," this fact is important. Indeed, in this book, I take no particular position as to what Paul means by tongues here or elsewhere. Paul's particular point at this stage in his argument works equally well no matter which view we take. He simply states that if people do not have a shared language, they cannot understand each other. If our churches only speak one language, we make the gospel foreign and incomprehensible to anyone in our city who does not speak our language. Intentionally or not, we lock them out of our church and erect a barrier between them and us. Every modern city and many modern towns are multilingual, but how many churches are?

> **If we live in multilingual cities and have monolingual churches, our practice does not line up with our confession.**

Every church I know would say that they are open to "whosoever will." Yet, if we live in multilingual cities and have monolingual churches, our practice does not line up with our confession. We leave it for someone else to reach and disciple these people with the gospel. We make linguistic difference a reason to exclude someone.

Every modern city and many modern towns are multilingual, but how many churches are?

Responding to Our Diverse Communities

How do churches respond to the growing multilingualism around them? In many cases, they don't. Go into many churches in Europe and North America and you will find a congregation full of people with the same skin color, the same language and most likely, the same kind of background. In fact, for a long time, this kind of homogenous church was the recommended strategy.

Experts in church growth used to talk about the "homogenous unit principle," which says that people "like to become Christians without crossing racial, linguistic or class barriers."[9] This makes sense. Most people naturally feel comfortable around those speaking the same language they do. We feel at home with people with whom we have shared experiences, stories, and identity.

---

9 Lausanne Committee for World Evangelization, "Pasadena Consultation," sec. 3.

If we are looking for churches to grow quickly, the homogenous unit principle can be a useful strategy. It has a lot in common with the secular field of marketing. But this strategy is destined to hit a wall.

Imagine a church that is built around the homogenous unit principle and aims to reach lawyers or university-educated people or young families. While this will work for a while, the reality of any major city is that, even if a church reached everyone in this group, it would eventually run out of people to reach. Even a large city can only have so many lawyers, university graduates, or even young families. What would happen when these lawyers turn into retired lawyers or when the young families become older families or grandparents?

Homogenous units are inherently limited. The people in these groups today will one day end up part of a different unit. Quite apart from the theological implications of sticking to our own little group (which we'll examine in the next chapter), the increasingly complex demographics of modern towns and cities make anything approaching the homogenous unit principle unsustainable.

No responsible church leader deliberately builds a church that keeps the gospel to their own little group. I do not believe for a minute that either church leaders or those who developed the homogenous unit principle used this tactic for malevolent reasons. It makes sense for churches to grow by adding people who are like those who already attend. Likewise, it makes sense that the first people added to a church will be those who share a background or a common interest with those already in the church. Yet, at some point, churches have to reach beyond these limits.

The demographic limitations of the homogenous unit principle might not be immediately apparent. After all, if a church is based in a particular community, it might feel normal for that community to be the immediate target. And, if that community happens to be relatively homogenous, then growth through homogeneity is going to look like it is working.

It is only when and if the community around us changes that we start to see why homogeneity is so limited. When that church in Wishaw (mentioned in the introduction) was first planted, it seemed that pretty much everyone spoke English as their first language and the biggest problems had to do with poverty. It seemed to make sense that a church there would grow primarily by being planted in a particular area and attracting the kinds of people who lived there. That meant that English was the language that mattered.

Yet, when I examined information on Wishaw now, I found out that more than 8 percent of school children in that town use a language other than English at home, with 38 different languages spoken.[10] This is in a town with just over 36,000 inhabitants. These children represent homes where English is not the primary language used. In these homes, people think and argue and play and express themselves in their own languages. If people are going to meet God, they will need to know that God speaks these languages too.

This story is repeating everywhere. While the homogenous unit principle sounds like a perfectly natural idea, it is powerless in the face of changing demographics, increasing migration, and the changes happening in our communities. This is before we even talk about changes in how we do church.

COVID-19 and the Always Open Church

None of these demographic or linguistic issues are particularly new. Sociologists, missiologists, church growth experts and even pastors have been saying for decades that demographic changes mean that churches are finding that their communities are changing around them. As far back as 1996, books started appearing to try to prepare churches for the leap to becoming multiethnic.[11] Sure, there were models and ideas and strategies floating around but one event changed the story completely.

During the global pandemic, most churches around the world shifted from meeting in-person to meeting online. This book is not the place for debates over the theological meaning of that, nor is this the right book to debate views on the rights and wrongs of those decisions. What is undeniable is that the pandemic brought about a seismic shift in how church services happened and, more importantly for this book, who could attend church.

The pandemic meant that the potential reach of a church was determined by the platform it used. Churches that decided to stay local and provide meetings over Zoom for their existing congregation could only reach those with the correct link for the meeting. The issue then was that churches had to decide whether to make the link public and possibly allow "Zoom bombing" where people could come in and disrupt the meeting. If they chose to make the link private, this made the church service only available to existing members of the church. This is hardly the most evangelistic decision possible.

Many churches chose to live stream their services on open, public platforms, such as YouTube, Facebook, or Vimeo. While this normally

---

10 North Lanarkshire Council, "Wishaw Community Profile."
11 One early example is Ortiz, *One New People*.

meant far less interaction than was possible on Zoom, as video was only sent in one direction, it did mean that, at least in theory, anyone could attend a church service anywhere in the world.

And people did attend. Secular British newspaper, *The Observer*, noted that a quarter of British adults watched or listened to a religious service during the pandemic, with 1 in 5 of those who tuned in having never visited a church before.[12] This is in a context where fewer people than ever in the UK are calling themselves Christian.[13] While the effects of the pandemic are still being played out in churches, the move to live streamed church opened the doors of the church to anyone who fancied trying to find a service.

Further, services were also available twenty-four hours a day, seven days a week anywhere in the world. The church I attend, which has around thirty people in attendance on a typical Sunday, saw one particular service viewed over 450 times. On a purely personal level, I was able to keep in touch with a church I used to attend in France, while my wife could watch services from that very same German church mentioned in the introduction.

We need to take time to reflect on what this means. There has been a lot of ink spilled on whether attending an online service can be seen as going to church, whether streaming a service creates a temptation for people to not ever attend in person, and on the nature of Christian fellowship. I will let others take part in those discussions, not because they aren't important but because they can deflect us from a few new realities.

The first reality is that whatever the rights or wrongs of streaming church services, they undeniably make church more accessible for people. Any church that is streaming can be watched around the world, as well as in the church nursery, and by members who cannot attend for some reason or another. The potential audience for such services is far larger than the people in the church. Done well, this presents real evangelism opportunities, even if the best way of inviting people off their sofas and into the sanctuary remains in question.

The second reality is that, now that pandemic restrictions have been eased around the world, streaming is optional. Many churches have decided that the end of the pandemic means the end of streaming. This is understandable, especially given limits on volunteer and staff time. While

---

12 Sherwood, "British Public Turn," 3.
13 Office of National Statistics, "Religion, England and Wales."

the technology has become more affordable and easier to use, it does still take a level of expertise to stream a service well.

There is nothing specifically wrong with deciding not to stream. Yet churches who have decided to continue streaming, and those for whom the pandemic simply meant continuing their previous technological activities, have much wider reach than those who did not. For those churches, the potential audience for their services is multicultural, multiracial, and multilingual—the kind of audience that was previously only found in a few large cities. The question is, what will they do to reach those people? In all of this, I am reminded of the words of John Wesley, who wrote in his diary:

> I look upon all the world as my parish; thus far I mean, that, in whatever part of it I am, I judge it meet, right, and my bounden duty to declare unto all that are willing to hear, the glad tidings of salvation.[14]

So where is the parish for your church? Every modern city is multilingual. The landscape of web streaming is multilingual. But how many churches are?

When I was growing up, it seemed reasonable for churches to think of their reach as being determined by geography, but that is no longer the case. Of course, churches are still called to love and serve specific geographic communities but now, with the touch of a button, that same church can simultaneously reach their own local community and anyone, anywhere with internet access. While many of those people might never step over the threshold of that church, they can be brought to faith, encouraged, and transformed by the words God is speaking thousands of miles away. The potential is there. It is up to us how it is used.

Reaching the World from Your Front Door

The thought of an always open, world-reaching church might seem idealistic or overwhelming. It is hard to imagine how a sermon delivered on a windy, rainy day in the west of Edinburgh might go on to transform lives in Kenya or Singapore. The possibility is there but, unless churches hear concrete stories of that possibility becoming real, it seems like mere fantasy.

Yet for many churches, reaching the world doesn't even require an internet connection. As was mentioned earlier in this chapter, many cities and even smaller towns now have multicultural populations. Add to this the numbers of international students, visiting workers, and refugees, and the

---

14 Wesley, *Journal of the Reverend*, 138.

harvest is great. This is all the more true when we realize that some of these people come from countries where evangelism is difficult or even banned.

As I was doing my PhD, I shared seminars with fellow PhD students in the same department who came from Greece, Egypt, China, and Syria. Churches who can reach student and visiting worker populations can reach countries where the door to Christianity is closed, simply by sharing the gospel with someone who is here temporarily. This is before we even consider the people who have moved here to work or seek asylum.

As churches reach their multicultural communities, they reach the world. In towns and cities around the world, churches now face a simple question: will you keep the riches of the gospel to people like you, even as the community changes around you, or will you take the opportunity to reach across barriers of culture, ethnicity, race, and language and in so doing, touch the whole world?

There is one final factor to consider. Churches and missions organizations often arrange conferences and large events. Does it make sense to have these in English only when we know that those attending will be coming from around the world? If we put on events aimed at international audiences but choose to keep those events in English when other options are available, what does that say about what we really think of our brothers and sisters in Christ around the world?

> *Will you take the opportunity to reach across barriers of culture, ethnicity, race, and language and in so doing, touch the whole world?*

To Whom Shall They Go?

So far, this chapter has covered changes in demographics, technology, and church practice. None of these are, by themselves, convincing enough to prove that churches in multilingual communities should be multilingual. Taking what was written about the town of Wishaw, for instance, I could just as easily focus on the 92 percent of people who do speak English at home and dismiss the 8 percent who don't.

A certain kind of logic allows us to argue that homogenous unit churches are fine, so long as there are enough of them to cover all the homogenous units in an area. Demographics alone don't prove that any specific church should become multilingual, even when its surrounding community is changing. In the same way, the growth of online church and the fact that it opens any church service to anyone could just as easily be seen as a reason why churches can get by just fine in English alone.

The most powerful arguments for multilingual church don't come from demographics—they come from theology, which will be covered in the next chapter. Paying attention to demographics can help us to understand some of the reasons that multilingual church is necessary. But, if we are to really get a feel for the power and potential of multilingual church, we have to turn these statistics and trends into real people, with faces, stories and feelings.

For people who do not speak the locally dominant language, the question really is "to whom shall we go?" Shall they go to a church that doesn't speak their language?[15] Shall they attend a church full of people just like them? Shall they just create a kind of church at home?

Building and maintaining multilingual churches doesn't just provide another church growth strategy. It provides a space where people can get used to their new country and still celebrate where they come from. At its best, multilingual church provides an open welcome to anyone, no matter their culture, nationality, or language. It is just as powerful for refugees looking for a place of safety and healing as it is for students and migrant workers looking for a place of peace and fellowship.

> *For people who do not speak the locally dominant language, the question really is "to whom shall we go?"*

While there are several models of multilingual church and a range of ways to offer language provision for people who need it, what they all have in common is a determination that language differences will not prevent people from being part of a church. Where communities are often divided by language differences, multilingual church turns those differences into the places where people meet each other and meet God, grow together, and demonstrate the barrier-breaking, people-reconciling love of God.

All around your church, you are likely to find people whose first language is not the language spoken in your church. What will you do to reach, teach, and disciple them?

Demographics offer some factual reasons why this kind of church is *useful*. Only the Bible can provide a vision of why this kind of church is *necessary*. It is to the Bible that we now turn.

---

15 Krihtova, "How to Enter the Church When the Door Is Closed," 41–51.

CHAPTER 2

Multilingual Church Is Biblical

It has always been on God's heart to create a reconciled, unified multiethnic family on earth, a creation only possible by Jesus the Messiah.[1]

The Destiny of Multilingual Church

There is one portion of Scripture that sums up the beauty and purpose of multilingual church better than any other. Let's start with multilingual heaven.

> After this I looked, and there was a great multitude that no one could count, from every nation, from all tribes and peoples and languages, standing before the throne and before the Lamb, robed in white, with palm branches in their hands. They cried out in a loud voice, saying,
>
> "Salvation belongs to our God who is seated on the throne, and to the Lamb!"
>
> And all the angels stood around the throne and around the elders and the four living creatures, and they fell on their faces before the throne and worshipped God, singing,
>
> "Amen! Blessing and glory and wisdom
> and thanksgiving and honor
> and power and might
> be to our God for ever and ever! Amen."
>
> Then one of the elders addressed me, saying, "Who are these, robed in white, and where have they come from?" I said to him, "Sir, you are the one that knows." Then he said to me, "These are they who have come out of the great ordeal; they have washed their robes and made them white in the blood of the Lamb.
>
> For this reason they are before the throne of God,
> and worship him day and night within his temple,
> and the one who is seated on the throne will shelter them.
> They will hunger no more, and thirst no more;
> the sun will not strike them,
> nor any scorching heat;

---

1 Gray, *High Definition Leader*, 147.

for the Lamb at the center of the throne will be their shepherd,
    and he will guide them to springs of the water of life,
  and God will wipe away every tear from their eyes."
(Rev 7:9–17, NRSV)

This picture of people from every nation, tribe, people, and language praising God together in the same place, after coming through suffering, is not just a picture of a heavenly reality but an inspiration for our earthly churches. We don't have to wait until heaven to experience a foretaste of this. We can have it right here when we partner with God to build, disciple and grow multilingual churches. When we pray "Your kingdom come. Your will be done, on earth as it is in heaven" (Matt 6:10 NRSV), we are praying for God to make our earthly reality reflect what is already true in heaven.

What is true in heaven is that people from every nation (or people group), every tribe, every people and language praise God, even when they haven't yet received everything God is going to do. In heaven, there are different languages, but there are no language barriers.

> **In heaven, there are different languages, but there are no language barriers.**

There are no in-groups and out-groups. There is no dominant people group, as all worship God. Only God can do this.

But that vision does not come out of nowhere. It comes at the end of a long and sometimes faltering story that covers almost the entire Bible. It represents the fulfilment of promises God made throughout the entire Old Testament. Those promises and that story give us the theological basis for multilingual church. Let's go back to where that story started.

Traces of Biblical Multilingualism

People are often surprised to find that multilingual ministry is in the Bible. Since we read the Bible in our own language, it is all too easy to forget the Bible was written in three languages: Hebrew, Aramaic, and Greek, and that the people in the Bible lived in multilingual societies. This necessarily meant that there were people interpreting (Gen 42:23; 2 Kgs 18:19–36) and that some people could speak more than one language (Dan 1:4; Acts 21:37–22:2).

This is more than just interesting context for our Bible readings. It means that the Bible we read was written in societies where migration and being multilingual were common, especially as large empires started to eat up more land. When an empire marches in, with its new customs, language, and culture, some kind of response is needed (Dan 1). Likewise,

Multilingual Church Is Biblical

when the call of God (Gen 12:1), family strife (Gen 27:41–28:2; 31:17–21), or forced exile (2 Kgs 17:6; 25:21b) mean that people must change where they live, they will have to find ways to adjust the language they use or learn a new one.

These are just some of the traces of migration and multilingualism in the Bible. The Pentateuch provides clear instructions about how to treat foreigners, implying that it was normal for people from one kingdom to find themselves in another. From the time of Babel, God spoke to people who lived in multilingual societies—societies in which various forms of migration took place. In that way, the varied contexts in which the Bible was written are not unlike our modern world. God is not in the least surprised that churches should find themselves in multilingual communities. It is how we respond to that fact that matters.

How Should People Hear?
Teaching in the Language People Speak at Home

Church interpreters and interpreting researchers have taken particular interest in one early example of multilingual worship. It comes hundreds of years before Jesus was born, at a time when it would seem unlikely that God would do something innovative.

In Nehemiah 8, we see the Jews in a rather precarious predicament. Yes, the walls around Jerusalem have been rebuilt. Yes, people are now moving into the city. But the people still lack something important. Waves of exiles have returned from Babylon but seventy years spent away from their homes and their previous culture and customs have muddied their memories as to who they are and what they are called to do. Their knowledge of their own religious festivals, the ones God ordained precisely to help them remember, are unclear at best.

They need a teacher. They have Ezra.

But Ezra has a problem. Jewish interpreting scholar, Francine Kaufman, explains it like this (my translation).

> In 538, the Edict of Cyrus permitted anyone who wished to return to their homeland. Most of these returning exiles no longer spoke any language but Aramaic, the diplomatic language of the Persian empire since the 5th century. In addition, a large Jewish community remained in Babylonia and constant exchanges, which would last for centuries, began between the Jews in Babylonia and those in Palestine.
>
> This bilingualism did not make Ezra's and Nehemiah's task any easier, as they sought to restructure the community in the

land of Israel. The temple was rebuilt but more than anything else, the emphasis was on relearning the tradition that had been lost in exile to an idol-filled country.[2]

There are a few important points to note about this account. The first is that, from the point of view of Ezra and Nehemiah, language was not the primary barrier to overcome, but rather, the people needed to rediscover who they are. The complexities of what languages people knew and could use parallels almost exactly their consciousness of who God has called them to be. Language reflects identity. That was true in Ezra's day, and it remains true now.

It is not that these people could not be true Jews unless they knew Hebrew and could read the Scriptures for themselves, just as we cannot say that someone cannot be a Christian without having a working knowledge of Hebrew, Aramaic, and Greek. Instead, what is important here is that the linguistic gap between the words people spoke and the words of the Torah represented a gap between who they had become in Exile and who God was calling them to be. To rediscover their identity, these people needed to understand what God was speaking to them.

Ezra's response is clear.

> Then Ezra opened the book in the sight of all the people, for he was standing above all the people; and when he opened it, all the people stood up. Then Ezra blessed the LORD, the great God. And all the people answered, "Amen, Amen!" with the raising of their hands; then they kneeled down and worshiped the LORD with their faces to the ground. Also Jeshua, Bani, Sherebiah, Jamin, Akkub, Shabbethai, Hodiah, Maaseiah, Kelita, Azariah, Jozabad, Hanan, Pelaiah, and the Levites explained the Law to the people while the people remained in their place. They read from the book, from the Law of God, translating to give the sense so that they understood the reading. (Neh 8:5–8, NASB)

The choice of Bible translation is important here. While many translations, such as the New Living Translation, New International Version, and New King James Version, tend to translate a certain Hebrew word as "gave the sense," the New American Standard Bible and the New Revised Standard Version translate the same word as "translated." To understand what is going on here, it helps to return to the research of Francine Kaufmann.

---

2 Kaufmann, "Contribution à l'histoire," 976.

But so that everyone could understand the meaning of the verses read, even the unlearned, women and children, he ensured that the Hebrew reading was accompanied by an oral translation into Aramaic. **This is, at least, the interpretation the Talmud gives to the word** *meforach* (which literally means, explicit, explained, interpreted) in the famous verse Nehemiah 8:8, "they read the book, in the Lord's Torah, *meforach*, so that the reading could be understood."[3]

Perhaps English-language Bible translators have differed in their translation of this word because it covers a broader range of meaning than any single English verb. Surely interpreting (in the sense used in this book), translating, explaining, and making explicit are all different things. While they may be distinct in English, in this passage they were simply different facets of the same practice.

This little point of disagreement is very meaningful for any discussion of a biblical view of multilingual church. The passage is about people relearning who they are through the practice that we might identify as "interpreting." Yet the more common view of interpreting found in much of Western thinking is that it is mostly about saying what the speaker said in another language, without any omission, explanation, or addition.[4] This suggests that interpreting doesn't include making something more explicit or explaining it.

Whatever it was that these Levites did for Ezra and the people listening, it was much more than what we often call "interpreting." Their primary concern was that people could understand and apply what they heard. Putting understanding and application first is a vital consideration for any multilingual church.

This priority leads to another very simple idea, which will be discussed more fully later. Our work to build and maintain multilingual churches will only succeed to the extent that we make multilingualism a central part of church life.[5]

A vital part of Ezra's work was addressing the multilingualism by providing a place where the Hebrew of the Bible could co-exist with the people's Aramaic. This wasn't just an attempt to bridge a temporary language gap but a deliberate decision that the word of God had to be

---

3 Kaufmann, "Contribution à l'histoire," 976.
4 See also Diriker, *De-/Re-Contextualizing Conference Interpreting*, vol. 53; Clifford, "Is Fidelity Ethical?" 89–114; and Downie, "Finding and Critiquing," 260–70.
5 See also, Downie, "Stakeholder Expectations"; Vigouroux, "Double-Mouthed Discourse," 341–69; Krihtova, "How to Enter," 41–51.

heard in the words people spoke every day. *God's word had to come to the people so that the people could understand again who they were.*

The context clearly supports this view. Reading the Torah in Hebrew and Aramaic led to celebration (Neh 8:12) and to the first festival of *Sukkoth*, or Shelters, since the exile (Neh 8:13–18). This wasn't simply a calendar co-incidence. Celebrating this festival helped people to remember the wanderings of their ancestors in the wilderness (Lev 23:42–43). These returned exiles were remembering and re-enacting who they were and where they came from. Hearing the word of God in their everyday language reminded them of the larger purposes of God and of their identity in that story.

From Multilingual Israel to Jesus, the King of All Nations

In Nehemiah 8, we see these returning Jews begin the process of rediscovering who they were by hearing the Torah in their language and applying it. This story repeats in much the same way throughout the Bible. Just as Jews had been scattered due to the Exile, so they would be scattered again throughout a different empire—the Roman one.

By the time we get to Acts, something brand new happens. In Ezra's day, the focus was still very much on meeting God at a specific time and place. Jerusalem was rebuilt precisely because it meant so much to Jewish identity and belonging. Prophets like Haggai and Malachi would directly link the building of the temple and the sanctification of temple worship to the building of the people and their holiness before God.

But with the coming of Jesus, the meaning of the temple changed. We don't have the space here for a thorough account of the relationship between Jesus and the temple or between early Christianity and temple worship. It is important, however, to note that Jesus's dire warnings about the temple (Matt 24:1–2; John 2:19) were used as evidence during his trial before the Sanhedrin (Matt 26:59–61). This trial ended in uproar when he announced clearly that "From now on, you will see the Son of Man sitting at the right hand of the Mighty One and coming on the clouds of heaven" (Matt 26:64b, NIV).

Jesus is choosing his words very carefully here. He is unmistakably alluding to the well-known Old Testament picture of the Son of Man who was given the right to judge and receive worship from "all people, nations, and languages" (Dan 7:14, NRSV) and claiming that identity for himself. There is also an important echo of his earlier self-revelation to Nathanael in John 1:51. In that verse, he tells Nathanael that "you will see heaven opened, and the angels of God ascending and descending upon the Son of Man."

This composite picture of Jesus as the son of man, upon whom angels ascend and descend and the one sitting at the right hand of the Mighty One, makes Jesus the new place where God and people meet, just as the temple was for the Jews before and after the Exile. But Jesus isn't just for the Jews, as the temple was. He judges and receives worship from everyone, everywhere, no matter their language, nation, people group, skin color, ethnicity, title, or background.

Before he ascended to heaven, Jesus twice commissioned his disciples to teach people everywhere about his kingdom in his power and authority (Matt 28:18–20; Acts 1:8). In short, in Christ, the doors to the kingdom have been flung open to "whosoever will" (cf. John 3:16), the veil has been torn (Matt 27:51), and the barriers between people groups have been destroyed (Eph 2:14). God has commissioned the church to reconcile people to himself and to each other (2 Cor 5:18–20; Eph 4; Phlm). Christ will be worshipped by a multilingual, multiethnic crowd. He claims the lordship of all nations. But what does that mean for individual churches?

Who Can Hear? Preaching to the Multilingual Crowd

Much of the New Testament covers how this works out in everyday church life. We should think through the importance of Acts 2 against this background of who Christ is and all he has commissioned us to do. In Acts 2, just like in Nehemiah 8, people have gathered for a Jewish festival. And just like in Nehemiah 8, there is a language barrier because of the effects of empire and conquest and some mix of forced and intentional migration. Just like in Nehemiah 8, God is doing something important and everyone needs to hear about it.

But unlike Nehemiah 8, there are several options on the table. Jews from around the empire and even the world had come to Jerusalem for the Festival of *Shavuot* or Weeks (Lev 23:15–22). This harvest festival took place fifty days after the first day of Passover, and would become the festival celebrating the giving of the Torah after the destruction of the temple in AD 70. Jews who were devout enough to come for this festival would almost certainly have had some Hebrew, even if it was mostly a liturgical language for them. If they were in regular contact with the Roman Empire or even Roman citizens, as some were, then they would have spoken Greek. Those from Judea and its surroundings would have also spoken Aramaic.

There were therefore three common languages or *linguae francae* that would have been perfectly acceptable for God to use to proclaim the new thing he was doing with the coming of the Holy Spirit. Yet a glance at the list of languages people heard when the Holy Spirit came so powerfully, a list that is so easy to miss, paints a very different picture:

> And at this sound the crowd gathered and was bewildered, because each one heard them speaking in the native language of each. Amazed and astonished, they asked, "Are not all these who are speaking Galileans? And how is it that we hear, each of us, in our own native language? Parthians, Medes, Elamites, and residents of Mesopotamia, Judea and Cappadocia, Pontus and Asia, Phrygia and Pamphylia, Egypt and the parts of Libya belonging to Cyrene, and visitors from Rome, both Jews and proselytes, Cretans and Arabs—in our own languages we hear them speaking about God's deeds of power." All were amazed and perplexed, saying to one another, "What does this mean?" (Acts 2:6–12, NRSV)

Check through the list and there is no mention of Greek, the language of empire and learning and no mention of Hebrew, the language of the Torah. In fact, verse 8 presents a perfect summary of the situation "we hear, each of us, in our own native language." The Greek word here is *dialektos*, the source of our word *dialect*. Everyone heard the word of God in their own dialect; not a trade language, not a lingua franca, not just the language of the region they happened to be in. Everyone heard in the language they knew best.

> **God ensured that the gospel was heard in local languages and dialects at a time when it wasn't absolutely necessary.**

We can understand this passage in two ways: (1) God empowered the disciples to be simultaneous interpreters; or (2) the Holy Spirit enabled people to hear in their own languages while the disciples spoke in spiritual tongues. In either case, the theological meaning is much the same. God ensured that the gospel was heard in local languages and dialects at a time when it wasn't absolutely necessary. God went far above and beyond what was strictly required to surprise, even astonish, people with an act of supreme love.

This love meant bringing the gospel to people in *their* languages, rather than waiting for them to learn new ones. People often argue that a translator "moves the reader to the author or the translator moves the author to the reader."[6] In Acts 2, God brings the gospel to the people in their language, rather than waiting for them to come to it in a language they have learned. This notion has rather obvious implications for Bible

---

6 Lindemann, "Friedrich Schleiermacher's Lecture," 115–22.

translation, but its most important implications in this book are those for multilingual churches.

If God prioritized local languages over the use of trade languages, why should we do anything else? At Pentecost we see a spectacular demonstration of God's own gospel strategy: do everything it takes to allow people to hear in the languages they use at home, in the marketplaces, among *their* people. Don't wait for people to come with a second language; reach them in their first language, the one that touches them most.

God's answer to the diversity of languages is not to somehow reverse Babel by making people speak a single language or a lingua franca. Neither does God nominate a language as a more special, holy language. Instead, God celebrates the diversity of languages by using all of them to allow people to hear the gospel. As spectacular as this demonstration was, there was still one issue. All the people who heard on that day were Jews, either born Jews or converts to Judaism. For the message to go to every nation, there were still two more steps needed.

Who Can Respond? Breaking Barriers ... Twice

Upon hearing the gospel in their dialects, the crowd in Acts 2 asked "what does this mean" (v. 12b). Peter responded using the writings of the prophet Joel, where it was promised that the Holy Spirit would be poured out on "all flesh" (Acts 2:17, citing Joel 2:28). This, he argued, was what God was doing right there, right then. Pentecost could not have been a complete fulfilment of that verse. All the people who heard on that day were Jews or proselytes attending a Jewish festival.

Within Peter's sermon to Jews was the seed of a much larger promise. It reflects God's promise to bless the whole earth through the descendants of Abraham (Gen 22:18). Consistent with Pentecost being the Festival of First Fruits, this particular gathering could only be the first sheaf of a much wider harvest.

We can see the first part of this wider harvest in Acts 8. At this point, the church has been mostly scattered by persecution—more migration!—which only served to help the gospel spread outside of Jerusalem and Judea to Samaria. After a revival in the region of Samaria, Philip receives a very odd instruction from God: move away from the crowds coming to salvation in Samaria and head down to a desert road. It made no sense. Here were thousands of people, newly saved and desperate for discipleship. Yet God calls a successful evangelist to leave all that behind and head where there were no people at all.

Well, there was one person. Riding hard, with sand spreading in all directions was a lone traveler—a eunuch from Ethiopia. We might know this story. It was a powerful encounter.

Eunuchs were forbidden from worshipping with God's people (Deut 23:1). No eunuch could become a priest, even if they were born into a priestly line (Lev 21:20). However, the prophet Isaiah had promised that the day would come when eunuchs would be welcomed to worship God (Isa 56:3–8).

What is intriguing about that passage in Isaiah is that it looked forward to a day when both eunuchs *and foreigners* would be accepted into God's people, as God would gather "the outcasts of Israel" (Isa 56:8a). In fact, this is exactly the chapter Jesus quoted when he cleansed the temple (cf. Matt 21:13), saying that God had intended it to be "a house of prayer for all the nations" (Mark 11:17b, NRSV).

The Isaiah passage means that all the nations would come to the temple to pray, not that the temple would be a place to pray for the nations who remained outside. God isn't just calling his people to be those who have a heart for the nations but to be those who pray physically alongside the nations.

It is impossible to understate just how much of a theological, practical, and political shift this was. Much of Jewish identity was based on their status as God's chosen people. This sustained them through persecution, exile, and now more persecution under the thumb of Rome. Paul explains in the book of Romans that identity based on chosen-ness could easily turn into an identity that assumed Jews were superior to the nations around them (see Rom 2). The promise that the temple would be a house of prayer for all nations was a promise that foreigners and outcasts would enjoy the same fellowship with God that Jews had. It was a promise that the temple, the place where God and humans met, was to be a place where all people who were dedicated to God would be welcome.

All people were to be invited to be God's people.

This promise is what we see beginning to unfold in Acts 8:26–40. Philip is called alongside a eunuch who held high office in the nation of Ethiopia but who could not, up until that point, have any real place among God's people, despite an obvious hunger to know God more. The fact that eunuch had the scroll of the prophet Isaiah (v. 30) shows just how desperate this eunuch was. Scripture scrolls were not a normal possession. Mostly, they were kept in synagogues and treated with the utmost respect, both because of their holiness and because they were expensive and time consuming to make—a complete Isaiah scroll would take around three days for a scribe to write.[7]

Philip started where the eunuch was (v. 35) and worked from there to a full understanding of what Jesus had come to do. This is again an

---

7 Millard, "Reading and Writing."

echo of God speaking to people in their *dialektoi*. That the eunuch was then baptized (vv. 36, 38), a sign of dying to his old identity and taking on Christ (cf. Col 2:12), shows more than just a wonderful response to the preaching of the gospel—Philip's willingness to baptize him (Acts 8:38) showed that this eunuch had received the promise of God: "I will give, in my house and within my walls, a monument and a name better than sons and daughters; I will give them an everlasting name that shall not be cut off" (Isa 56:5, NRSV).

True, this man was both a eunuch and a foreigner, but he was obviously someone who was close to Judaism. Could God save *other* foreigners? Could God even save people who oppressed Israel?

It would take only two more chapters for the book of Acts to get an answer but seven more for the church to grasp its meaning.

If there was a formidable cultural barrier in the time of the early church, it was the barrier between the Jews and the Romans who oppressed them. Until the destruction of the temple in AD 70, Jews held different views about how they should relate to Rome. Some people favored co-operating with the Empire, others distancing yourself from it by living as far away from it as possible or by keeping the Law as studiously as possible, while others looked for a way to oppose it, with violence if necessary.

This barrier explains why it would take a triple vision (Acts 10:9–15) for Peter, the same Peter who preached boldly on Pentecost, to be persuaded to proclaim the gospel somewhere completely new: the household of a Roman officer. To understand how significant breaking this barrier was for the church (and for us), it is worth quoting Peter himself:

> He said to them, "You yourselves know that it is unlawful for a Jew to associate with or to visit a Gentile; but God has shown me that I should not call anyone profane or unclean. So when I was sent for, I came without objection. Now may I ask why you sent for me?" (Acts 10:28–29, NRSV)

God had asked Peter to do something his culture and training told him he shouldn't do. We won't find the prohibition Peter talks about anywhere in the Old Testament. It was his upbringing, not the Scriptures, that told him Gentiles were unclean. After all, God had promised to bless the whole earth through Abraham's descendants (Gen 22:18) and God had prohibited the Jews from mistreating foreigners in their land (Exod 22:21; 23:9). In fact, Jesus own bloodline includes Rahab, the Canaanite, and Ruth, the Moabite (Matt 1:5).

Peter here is beginning to learn that God's promise was to separate the Jews to be "light to the nations" (Isa 49:6, NRSV, cf. Rom 2:19) and that that light shone through Jesus. Put simply, Peter was realizing that salvation through Jesus was open to anyone who would accept it. There were no more barriers of language, culture, race, or ethnicity. By baptizing Cornelius's household in the Spirit (Acts 10:44), God proved incontrovertibly that he accepted all people who would follow him. Yet that act would prove highly controversial.

Whom Do We Allow to Hear? Applying God's Open Invitation

By this point in Acts, God has pulled down any remaining linguistic and ethnic barriers that could prevent someone from hearing the word and accepting the lordship of Christ. First, God showed that linguistic differences were not to be removed by the use of a single, especially chosen "holy language." Everyone heard the gospel in their own, local languages in Acts 2. Next, by sending Philip to preach to the Ethiopian eunuch, God showed that old barriers, including ethnicity or damage to the body, were no longer valid. Finally, God now summarily dismissed any power and status barriers by sending Peter to preach to the household of Cornelius, an act which shows that the old "dividing wall" (Eph 2:14) was now broken.

The question is no longer whether God wants all people to hear the gospel in their own language, but how will the church engage in that process? It is one thing for people to go on a mission trip, deliver the gospel to some faraway place and come home with an interesting story. It is quite another thing when this radical commitment to declaring the gospel across languages and cultures becomes the reality in our local church. How do we respond when what God is doing begins to have real effects on what we are called to do?

The early Church faced that question too, as it went from being mostly Jewish, with a few gentile converts, to accepting substantial numbers of gentiles. This might have modern parallels in churches today as they begin to welcome people from different social and cultural backgrounds. In the case of the salvation of Cornelius, it was evidence of the Holy Spirit at work that convinced the Jerusalem church that it was God who was extending the boundaries of who could be accepted as members of God's people (Acts 11:18). Might the same evidence be important in our churches?

As work among the gentiles continued, tensions returned. It is helpful to be reminded that this work, which really got going with the sending of Paul and Barnabas (Acts 13:1–3) was not just crossing one boundary but many different cultural and linguistic ones (see Acts 14:11–13). It is against this backdrop that we should read the Jerusalem Council in Acts 15. While we might read it as a mostly theological debate about adherence to the Jewish Law, with almost two thousand years of history between us and them, it was primarily a discussion about what it meant to belong to the Church, to be part of God's people. Did becoming a Christian mean leaving behind prior cultural identities and practices to take on Jewish ones?

Does joining our church today mean that people have to speak the same language as the rest of the church? Do we think that if people are going to come to a church in an English-speaking country, they should have to learn English? If people are going to come into our church, it stands to reason that they should take on the culture and practices of the church, right? Viewed through this lens, multilingual church is a long road towards integrating people to become more like us. Indeed, one contributor to a book on intercultural church specifically recommends that people not stay in home groups for people from their cultural background too long, so they can be better integrated into the "wider church."[8]

Yet the Jerusalem Council ruled against that approach.

> For it has seemed good to the Holy Spirit and to us to impose on you no further burden than these essentials: that you abstain from what has been sacrificed to idols and from blood and from what is strangled and from fornication. If you keep yourselves from these, you will do well. Farewell. (Acts 15:28–29, NRSV)

This is a vital theological point: we do not need to follow the Law to follow Jesus. It is also a vital point for multilingual church. Aside from requiring the gentile believers to avoid behavior that would offend Jews and damage relationships, this letter invites gentile believers into a place where their identity is found in their relationship with Christ. In other words, they were invited to be who God called them to be within their culture, rather than being required to take on a new one. Since God was welcoming them into fellowship with him, we should welcome them into fellowship with us.

Theologically, this opened the floodgates for gentile believers and was foundational for the doctrine of salvation by grace through faith. In terms of multilingual church, this finding means that multilingual church cannot be a temporary stage on the way to people being forced to become more like us. Multilingual church is not about making people more like us but

---

8 DeYmaz and Li, *Leading a Healthy*, 155.

about allowing people to hear what God is saying so they can become more like Christ.

For this reason, Paul could declare that "there is no longer Jew or Greek, there is no longer slave or free, there is no longer male and female; for all of you are one in Christ Jesus." (Gal 3:28 NRSV). While it would seem easy to make this simply a point about salvation, Paul's context is much wider. He criticizes Peter's decision to stop eating with gentiles (Gal 2: 11-14) as it recreated a division in the church that God had deliberately erased. Paul is arguing that churches should not allow any practices that would see one group in the church elevated over another. For him, there can be no in-groups, no exclusion based on language or culture, and no calls for people to become like some larger crowd in the church, especially if what matters is "faith working through love" (Gal 5:6b, NRSV).

The theological question about *how* we are saved determines our status in the church and questions any attempt to make or maintain one culture as dominant. As Peter put it earlier "If then God gave them the same gift that he gave us when we believed in the Lord Jesus Christ, who was I that I could hinder God?" (Acts 11:17, NRSV)

Giving a biblical account of multilingual church should therefore challenge our motives and aims. We should not provide language services so people can better integrate into the church, but so that they can hear the word of God and become more like Christ. If the goal of the church is to enable people to become like Christ together and if we work towards helpful ways of welcoming people, then the integration should come anyway and will be a two-way process. People who speak different languages are integrated into the church as the church integrates the theological, practical, and leadership realities of being multilingual into its identity and practice. This was the experience of the early church, as it dealt with issues such as multilingual food distribution (Acts 6:1–7), rethinking theology in light of God's radical acceptance of people from different backgrounds (Acts 10–11; 15; Gal), and creating space for the gifts God has given to be used in the church (Rom 12).

> **Multilingual church is not about making people more like us but about allowing people to hear what God is saying so they can become more like Christ.**

It is that vision of people who speak different languages learning, serving, and growing more like Christ together that leads us to the picture of multilingual heaven that started this chapter. It is that vision that justifies multilingual church. But how does that vision become reality?

The rest of this book will examine different approaches that churches can use. We will not shy away from the challenges and risks of each of these approaches. We will also address the human effort it takes to build, disciple, and grow multilingual churches. In the end, however, this is God's vision, not just ours. We till the ground and sow the seed but it is only God who can give the increase.

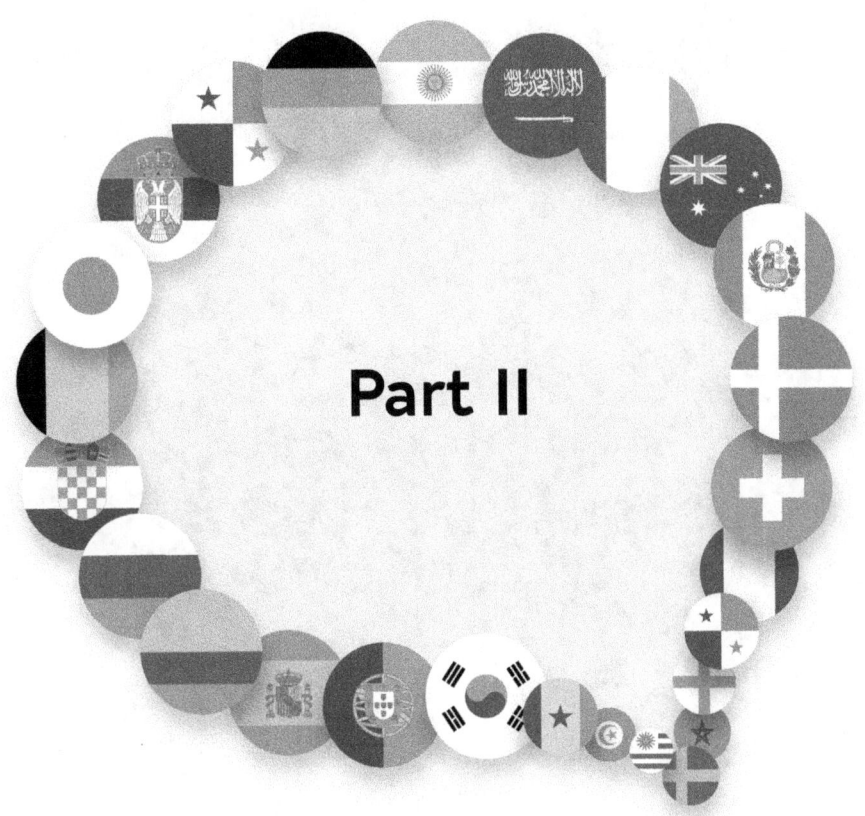

Part II

Common Ways to Do Multilingual Church

CHAPTER 3

They'll All Learn Our Language Anyway

Over the next seven chapters, I want to examine different approaches churches have to multilingualism and where they lead. More often than not, these approaches are linked to specific ways of responding to multilingualism in our communities. Chapter 12 covers the more technical details of the different solutions churches can use and how they work.

For the moment, I want us to consider what it feels like to experience different approaches to multilingual church and what they say about both our churches and, more fundamentally, our hearts. The first approach is the simplest: do nothing at all. What if they just assume that people will learn the locally dominant language, so language provision is not needed?

Does It Make Biblical Sense to Do Nothing?

At this point, it is helpful to use our imaginations. Imagine if some missionary families had been away from your church for decades, without returning back home. They have been in a country where your language is not spoken and so have gotten used to working, shopping, reading, and thinking in another language. Their children even speak the other language, not the common language of your church. The adults, while technically still first language speakers of your language, have experienced language attrition.[1] Their skills in your language are not nearly as strong as they used to be.

How should a church leader respond to this situation?

One approach is to simply resign ourselves to the fact that these people will soon regain their language. Their kids will have to work on their language skills to fit in, and church should be a good environment for that to happen. The logical thing then is to do nothing. Let the families settle back into hearing your language. Let their kids work out how to understand people. Be part of the integration process by doing nothing at all.

This response might sound odd, yet it happens in many churches today. The logic of "they'll learn our language anyway" prevails over thoughts of allowing people to encounter God in their heart language. Churches can conduct language classes but not adjust their services. They might arrange activities but not think of how people will experience them in a

---

1 Keijzer, "Regression Hypothesis," 9–18.

foreign language. They can provide aid but not consider through how to communicate with the people receiving it.

If Ezra had followed this logic in Nehemiah 8, he would have arranged for Hebrew lessons for the returning exiles, arguing that, since they now lived in Israel, they should learn Hebrew. He would have explained to them that learning the language of Scripture is an important spiritual discipline with real benefits. He would have done his readings in Hebrew and left it at that.

We know from Scripture that he did none of those things. Yes, he read the Scriptures in Hebrew but the Levites offered a clear, understandable version of what was read in Aramaic. Remember, the exiles who returned either no longer spoke Hebrew or had lost fluency over time, especially since the exile had lasted seventy years. This is more than enough time for a generation to get rusty in their Hebrew while the next perhaps never learns it at all.[2]

Such interpreting not only aimed at rendering Hebrew words into Aramaic but doing so in a way that everyone could understand, no matter their age, gender, or education.[3] Ezra didn't wait for people to understand Hebrew before opening the Scriptures to them; he made sure they heard God's message in the languages they already used.

Some see Nehemiah 8 as an example of good preaching,[4] but it is primarily an example of what the Bible asks leaders to do when faced with differences in language, education, or culture. Just as Jesus came down to us, speaking and acting in ways we could understand, we too are called to communicate with people in ways they can understand.

Yes, there will still be moments of confusion. Yes, not everything Jesus said or did was understood by the people around him. Yet Jesus did use images, parables, and analogies so that people would understand. Reading through the Gospels gives us many examples of Jesus switching the way he speaks according to his audience. He could just as easily theologically joust with the Pharisees and Sadducees as he could talk to the crowds about how much God cares for them, using examples from flowers or farming. When people misunderstood Jesus, it was about the state of their heart, not the language Jesus spoke (Matt 13:11–13). Jesus's parables explained the kingdom through everyday realities.

---

2 Portes and Schauffler, "Language and the Second," 650–51; Portes and Hao, "E Pluribus Unum," 275 both report language loss within a single generation and that languages can be totally lost within three generations of a family changing country.

3 Kaufmann, "Contribution à l'histoire," 976.

4 Kuruvilla, *Text to Praxis*, 151–54.

Those who grasped their meaning were not those who took pride in their education or their prior knowledge but rather those who wanted to learn humbly and follow him.

Do Unto Others

As chapter 1 explains, the number of people who change countries is growing. For many churches, the challenge might be to meet the needs of international students at a nearby university. For some, migrant workers might make up a good proportion of the population. Still others might be confronted with a substantial population of refugees. There are even churches in established bilingual or trilingual communities or countries. What should these churches do?

Using the "they'll all learn our language anyway" approach would look something like this:

A visitor arrives in the church. They walk in the door and have no idea what the greeter on the door is saying, so they nod politely. They find a seat, only for someone to gesture at them and utter words that mean nothing to them. The visitor then finds another seat and is confronted by songs they don't understand, followed by announcements that sail over their head. If they stay long enough for the sermon, they will still leave with no idea who anyone is or what anyone tried to communicate. What is the chance that they will come back?

Even if they have some skills in the locally dominant language, they'll likely miss the majority of what goes on. They might recognize the odd song and manage to sing along, but the whole experience will be more like watching an old TV that wasn't properly tuned in than meeting with God. Once again, what are the chances that they will come back?

In both cases, there is an even more important question to answer: what will that experience say to visitors about how much we care for them? We can have all the clever signs and smart websites we want, but if people turn up and feel like they don't belong, they will simply stop coming. Even worse, the way we treat visitors is a reflection of how we believe God sees them. Who would be interested in following a God who speaks a language you don't understand and expects you to figure things out for yourself? Will anyone take seriously our message about God's love when we do nothing to help them to hear it in a way they can understand?

There is a rather theological-sounding retort to all of this. Someone could read all this and say, "Isn't it God's job to help people understand? If the Holy Spirit wants people to understand, can't he make them understand, just like Pentecost?"

It is true that God is free to allow anyone to understand at any time. But God is also free to feed anyone with food from the sky at any time. Yet, churches still create soup kitchens and have fellowship meals. God is free to speak to anyone through the Word at any time, yet we still have preaching. God is free to supernaturally transport people from place to place, like he did with Philip the evangelist, yet we still board trains, planes, and automobiles.

When it comes to the logic that visitors will have to learn our language at some point anyway, the issue is not God's power but our own hearts. God can do miracles. God still does miracles. Yet we would question the theology of anyone who tried to get round the biblical imperative of giving to the poor by saying, "God promised to provide for the poor, so Christians don't need to care for them."

The same principle applies to the question of what to do about language differences among people in our churches. God can make people understand anything at any time. But God also calls us to put in the effort to do what he has empowered us to do. Appealing for believers to actively reach the people in their communities who speak different languages does not in any way reduce God's sovereignty; it simply reminds us of our responsibility.

Jesus told us to "do to others as you would like them to do to you" (Luke 6:31, NLT). As someone who has been blessed to travel to different countries, I am all too aware of the difference it makes when someone explains the information I need in the languages I speak. If I appreciate the effort people put into learning English or French and the impact their work has on me, why would I want to deny others of that impact?

For varied reasons, some people prefer to converse, go to church, and even sing in their second or third language. Some people want church to be a place where they learn the languages and customs of a country.

The "they'll learn our language" attitude places the burden on other people and on God; it absolves us of responsibility.

It is important, however, not to assume that this desire is universal or that we don't need to bother offering language assistance. The key factor is not the preferences of a single group but what our approaches say about our hearts. In part 3 of this book, we will look in detail at how to find out what language provision is needed and wanted among groups in the church.

The "they'll learn our language" attitude places the burden on other people and on God; it absolves us of responsibility. It shows little love and little interest in others' needs. It is hard to make that reasoning work in the light of Jesus who told us to do to others as we would like them to do to us. It is even harder to make sense of that position in light of a God who went out of his way to come to earth and die in our place.

The Truth about "They'll Learn Our Language Anyway"

Whenever we rely on other people's language learning rather than making our churches truly open to everyone, we send a message that we care more about what is comfortable for us than about reaching people who need Jesus. That message may not be a true reflection of our hearts, but it's the message people receive. "They'll learn our language anyway" is a heart position more than it is a theological one. Conversely, when we put in effort and take time to help people grasp God's message in their languages, we tell them with our actions that there is a God who wants to be known by them. We create space where they feel truly welcome.

There are, of course, good reasons why churches can't or won't offer some kind of language provision. Sometimes, there is the issue of knowledge. Not everyone knows how to set up ways for people to participate in their own language. That kind of thing gets complicated quickly.

Some churches simply don't need to become multilingual. There are still areas where everyone speaks the same first language. While migration is growing, it hasn't touched everywhere equally. If there is no need on the ground for multilingual church, it is perfectly fine not to provide it.

Some churches lack the capacity to become multilingual, even if they want to. Around the world, there are house churches, small missional communities, and all sorts of small-scale gatherings. There are other churches where leaders and volunteers are already stretched to breaking point. Adding something else would simply be too much.

Sometimes it is fine to do nothing. Not all churches need to become multilingual. Not all churches can be multilingual. Not all churches should be multilingual.

Yet when churches who could be multilingual decide not to be, it should give us pause. If a church meets in a multilingual community, yet everyone in the church speaks the same language, it means that some group is being excluded, either accidentally or deliberately. If the gospel we preach is not reaching all kinds of people in our communities, or if it only brings in people like us, we should ask some hard questions.

Saying "they'll all learn our language anyway" is not a statement about the location or capacity of the church. It is a statement about the intention and the heart of the church. It says that, even if some kinds of people want to come, we will not welcome them. We stand with arms folded while the world around us cries out for help and for Jesus.

"They'll all learn our language anyway" isn't about "them" at all. It's about us.

The Extent of Our Love

There is a time and a place for monolingual church. There are legitimate reasons for a church to offer language lessons. There are also legitimate reasons not to become multilingual. There are, however, good reasons to question, if not entirely reject, the view that "they'll all learn our language" so we don't need to help people understand.

How we respond to the needs around us demonstrates how much we love people and how much we love God. Just as James 3:14–17 challenges us to put our faith into action with how we treat people with physical needs, we are challenged to put our faith into action in how we treat people with language needs.

Our response to the language needs of our communities is a direct reflection of our love. The people we meet will read our response in those terms. Just as Ezra and Nehemiah arranged for everyone to hear the Torah in a language they understood and in a way that made sense to them, so we must be ready, when the need arises, to make the same effort. The same God who laid everything down to reach us might just call your church to pay the price to reach the multilingual communities around you. In the next chapter, we will look at some helpful ways to do just that.

CHAPTER 4

Add Services in Different Languages?

If doing nothing but leaving people with the burden of learning the locally dominant language and trying to fit in is uncaring and unbiblical, surely setting up church services in their language is a perfect solution, right?

Whenever church people find out what I do, there are several responses. First, they agree that the idea of multilingual church is interesting. But it is also surprisingly common to hear that a church has a service in another language or shares their building with some kind of migrant church. In fact, I have even heard it said that creating different church services for different languages is the ideal.

Compared to the problematic thinking behind assuming people should just learn the locally dominant language, the idea of different services in different languages seems quite good. If we assume that people prefer to worship with people who are like them,[1] then creating church meetings where people all speak the same language seems to be a useful tool. In fact, it is not unusual to hear services in different languages mentioned in books that aren't even about multilingual church at all.[2]

But do such services deserve the popularity? What happens to churches that start running services in different languages or who work with other churches to do the same thing?

What It Looks Like to Have Different Services in Different Languages

There are a variety of ways to approach offering services in different languages. There are some great books that cover each of the models at a depth that I couldn't possibly imitate here.[3] However, we can broadly split these models into three categories.

Category 1: The Rental Model

In the rental model, a migrant church simply rents space from a church that has a building and holds services of their own in the relevant language. This approach can make a lot of sense for both churches.

---

1 Hayward and McGavran, "Without Crossing Barriers?" 203–24.
2 For example, see Peter Scazzero, *Emotionally Healthy Spirituality*, 18.
3 Ortiz, *One New People*; Garces-Foley, *Crossing the Ethnic Divide*, 155–57.

The migrant church can be assured that they are renting from people who know all about the requirements of having a church. The church with the building can gain some much-needed cash.

Neither church is required to make any great changes or sacrifices. As long as the service times line up, chairs are left in the right place, and rooms are clean and tidy, there is unlikely to be any real tension. In addition, the church with the building can feel that they are doing something to reach people from a different background, with a minimum of initial effort.

Needless to say, the rental model has some significant drawbacks. The fact that it doesn't ask either church to make any real adjustments means that it is as much a commercial arrangement as it is a spiritual one. While this is not necessarily wrong, it is important for us to remember that simply renting out space is not an effective way for a church to reach a community. At best, it can support existing work among that community.

The second drawback explains why this kind of commercial relationship cannot be seen as a way of reaching a community. The rental model does not encourage churches to work together beyond the most basic level of coordinating service times. Realistically, what this model creates is two separate churches who happen to have a financial relationship with each other. Unless something else brings them together, it is quite likely that the relationship will simply not last. The church with the building might decide to stop renting out space for whatever reason, or the church renting space might outgrow the agreement.

As financially helpful as the rental model can be, and however much it might suit some churches, it simply isn't reasonable or honest to call it a multilingual church. It might help introduce two churches to each other but that's about it. It can be a place to start, but there are deeper, more helpful models.

Category 2: The Space-Sharing Model

I had never even heard of the space-sharing model until I started my PhD. While trying to get my head around different ways to understand church interpreting, I read the research of Jennifer Rayman. I was specifically struck by one article on how a sermon was interpreted from American Sign Language into English at the dedication of a single building shared by two congregations: one hearing and one Deaf.[4]

---

4 Rayman, "Visions of Equality," 73–114.

Add Services in Different Languages?

The interpreting itself is fascinating and is something that church interpreting experts[5] have spent time discussing. While the interpreting in that article is fascinating, what matters much more in the context of this chapter is why the interpreting was needed at all and what that tells us about churches that share space but still exist as separate congregations.

Here is the setup. There were two congregations using the same building. In this case, we don't have one church renting from another, but two congregations who meet at the same time in different rooms. Over time, this arrangement became more complicated. The congregations spent three years in one building, which they rented together, but didn't physically have the space to meet together. But now, to the joy of both churches, the two congregations can buy their own building.[6]

After buying their own building, the congregations can move in and meet at the same time once again. To celebrate, they have a joint building dedication. At this dedication, Dr. Francis J. Casale, the senior pastor of the Deaf congregation, is invited to speak. Since this was a service with both Deaf and hearing people present, interpreting was needed from American Sign Language into English.

The interpreter found herself in a tricky position. She felt that it was normal in the culture of the Deaf church to talk about what it means to be Deaf in the USA, as opposed to being hearing[7] and to carefully use labelling to sort people into three clear groups: Deaf, hearing, and interpreters.[8] Yet the interpreter felt that such labelling created exclusion. This same labelling, which was completely unknown in the hearing congregation, was a key structural point in the sermon Dr. Casale delivered.[9] This sermon clearly pointed out how the Deaf community had often been oppressed by hearing people but how the relationship between the Deaf and hearing pastors was a wonderful example of how something better was possible.

To sum up, here is an interpreter at an important event. They are required to interpret a sermon based on an idea they disagree with, to a congregation who had never come across that idea before and who are quite likely to be offended by it, even if the sermon was going to get to a happy conclusion. How the interpreter dealt with that situation is

---

5 Hokkanen, "To Serve," 18; Balci Tison, "Interpreter's Involvement," 22; Downie, "Stakeholder Expectations of Interpreters," 68–69.
6 Rayman, "Visions of Equality," 74.
7 Rayman, 76.
8 Rayman, 86–87.
9 Rayman, 76–85.

a story for another day. The fact that sticky situation ever existed says something important about what happens when congregations with different languages share space.

Simply being in the same building at the same time is not enough to build unity. Simply sharing mortgage payments and having leaders who meet together is not enough to make the arrangement work. Where churches share space but have different languages and cultures, there will always be the potential for cultural conflicts, such as the one that the interpreter had to deal with.

Space-sharing is good, but it creates as many problems as it solves. The question isn't so much about which church meets where and when, but how they build real, deep unity. For the congregations to walk together consistently and effectively in true unity, for them to truly be a multilingual church, they must take their relationship a step further.

Category 3: Joint Leadership

The more closely churches with different languages and cultures work together, the trickier things become. The idea of having different services in different languages is appealing in its simplicity. You keep your English service as it is right now and create a time and a space for a Spanish service, or a French service, or an Arabic service. Once that is done, you have a multilingual church and that's it, right?

Well, not quite. It has to be admitted that, even among some experts, the different services in different languages approach is the only model of multilingual church given any real attention.[10] The most obvious risk with this setup is that the members of each congregation simply end up drifting apart, as they end up associating more with their linguistic and cultural identity than they do with the wider church of which they are supposed to be part.

One answer to this would seem to be to double-down on the idea of there being a single church identity.[11] What if, for example, there was some kind of co-ordination as to the sermons being preached, the songs being sung and even the ministries being set up? This might foster a real sense of unity. Alternatively, it might just feel like the dominant church, let's say the English-speaking one, pushing its views of preaching, worship, and ministry onto people who have very different ideas.

To avoid any sense of spiritual oppression, some churches might instead opt for a shared, multicultural, or even multilingual leadership

---

10 Garces-Foley, *Crossing the Ethnic Divide*, 156.
11 Marti, "Fluid Ethnicity," 11–16.

team. This could reduce any sense of one congregation forcing its will onto others and could encourage some shared meetings or some cross-fertilization of ideas across all the congregations.

Yes, this is indeed much better than any alternative we have seen so far and goes some way towards fixing some of the problems that come whenever a church tries the "different services in different languages" model. It reduces the chance of the different congregations simply wandering away from each other, reduces the likelihood of one congregation imposing its will on another, and should help to create a sense of shared identity.

But how far down will this unity trickle?[12] Seen from the perspective of the leadership, it would be clear that this is one church, which happens to meet in different languages. Seen from the perspective of a member or even a visitor, this is simply a church that meets in the language they use. They could quite easily go from cradle to grave and hardly even be aware that the services in other languages existed, let alone ever meet someone who attends one.

> **No arrangement with different services in different languages ever asks people to meet with those from different cultures.**

Ironically, even with the best possible shared leadership, running multiple services in various languages will end up with the same fundamental challenge as can be found in the rental model. No arrangement with different services in different languages ever asks people to meet with those from different cultures. None of these arrangements ever ask people to make any changes to how things are done or to how they act in church to welcome people who are different. Church goes on exactly as it has before and the whole idea of reaching our multilingual communities is delegated to another congregation.

No matter how carefully the leaders share the load and welcome each other, for as long as the services simply run in one language each, no one in the congregation is ever asked to echo the shared ideals of the leaders. The idea of multilingual church in such cases is more of a leadership ideal than a weekly reality.

This is all a reflection of the model itself. These issues arise before we even ask where churches are supposed to find the right leaders to

---

12 This question was an important aspect of the DMin work of Robert G. Perez, who worked on introducing this model into the church he led. The churches ended up growing further apart, rather than closer together, possibly due to problems with generating trust across the two leadership teams. See Perez, "Generating Trust," 119–24.

make the model work. Once such leaders have been found, how then can they be nurtured to the point that the leaders of say, the Spanish-speaking congregation, share equal seniority with the leaders of say, the English-speaking congregation, even if those congregations attract different numbers of people and thus pull in different amounts of money and resources? How can leaders resolve budgetary tensions in a way that doesn't make one set of leaders feel less than others?

Yes, the shared leadership model is probably the ideal way of making services in different languages work but the whole idea of different services in different languages is problematic. If the problems of different services in different languages don't seem that pressing, it is worth thinking through what it would feel like for people attending the church.

The Visitor Experience

Imagine that you are a visitor to a church. Maybe you are on holiday. Maybe you have been forced from your home, due to circumstances outside your control. Maybe you are just taking a break for a week. You look up a church online. It seems good so you decide to pay a visit.

At the door, you are met by someone who doesn't speak your language. They look at you confused and eventually, in a mixture of vague gestures and the odd word in your language, they explain to you that this isn't *your* service. *Your* service, the one in your language, is in three hours. It might also be in a different part of the building. They don't know. They only know *their* service, which is starting right now. Would you bother coming back to *your* service?

That kind of greeting wouldn't feel very welcoming. It wouldn't feel like outreach. It certainly wouldn't feel like you were valued or important. Isn't the gospel supposed to be for everyone? Isn't church supposed to love and welcome everyone?

The truth is, when we separate people into different services in different languages, we inadvertently create spaces that exclude people. Yes, we might say that we are including them by having services in their own languages, but the reality is that we are excluding them from other services. For every space we make for a language, we close off one by having a service that is inaccessible otherwise. Different services in different languages is an exclusion and sorting strategy as much as it is an inclusion and welcoming strategy.

This applies no matter how well different services in different languages is done. In the rental model, the problem for visitors is quite acute as *their* service might be entirely different to the service in the other language. People might arrive looking for a charismatic church and find that the service in their language is High Anglican or vice-versa. It has to be said, however, that visitors are less likely to be confused in the rental model as the two congregations are clearly two different churches, with their own advertising, websites, and perhaps even bulletin boards.

Conversely, the problem of seeming exclusion is more subtle in the space-sharing model. With clear signage and services at the same time, people are at least likely to find their service with minimal fuss. But the two congregations are still different congregations, meeting in different rooms. True, it might be possible to use tea and coffee time to bring the two together but that might not be enough. By having two separate services in two different rooms, we are making a statement that underlines the differences between the congregations, not their oneness in Christ.

The joint leadership model does not solve the problem either. If the services run at different times, there will be those awkward moments when people turn up at the wrong time for their service. If the services run at the same time, the visitor experience is essentially the same as in the space sharing model. Having joint leadership does not make much of a difference to the experience of visitors, nor does it fundamentally change the symbolism of having different congregations, using different languages, meeting in different spaces, or at different times.

The Pros and Cons of Different Services in Different Languages

It will come as no surprise, given the previous discussion, that having different services in different languages should not be seen as ideal. It does have some advantages, but its disadvantages should give leaders pause.

Let's start with the advantages. Firstly, creating space, any space, for people to experience God in their own language is preferable to the glib platitudes we use when we just expect people to learn the local language. Doing something is always better than doing nothing. Having different services in different languages can be a way of reaching diverse communities.

As soon as we create a space for people, we tell them that they are invited, valued, and welcome. And there can be few deeper ways of welcoming people than by creating a space where their language is heard, seen, and sung. Of course, people will feel more valued when they hear their language spoken. Creating spaces for that can also make it easier for people to build friendships and community.

Different services in different languages can and probably do help to build relationships and community. They should, if done well, build an environment where people feel free to worship in a way that means the most to them. If for no other reason than that, doing something in other languages should always be high on the agenda of any church that seeks to be multilingual.

Yet it is undeniable that when we create different services in different languages, we build up as many barriers as we tear down. We tell our congregants and the world around that it is okay to see languages as badges of separation. We, hopefully inadvertently, preach theologies that prize monolingualism over a diversity of languages and sameness over difference. The greatest danger of this model is precisely that it does not require any changes in our thinking, theology, or practice. Church goes on as normal and no one is ever put in a position where they have to cross cultural or language barriers.

> **The greatest danger of this model is precisely that it does not require any changes in our thinking, theology, or practice.**

The advantages of having different services in different languages should be enough to tell us that there is something helpful about this model that we need to retain. The disadvantages and the inadvertent exclusion the model creates should warn us that it certainly is not enough on its own. It is not an ideal way of running Sunday services.

If we can't separate people out by language every Sunday, how can we cope with having different languages in our churches? In the next chapter, we will discuss some ways that different languages can be woven into the same church service.

CHAPTER 5

Different Languages, One Service

I didn't expect to experience multilingual worship at an academic conference on Bible translation. But there I was, attending online like everyone else and experiencing a little touch of multilingual heaven. To begin the conference, a group of musicians from a ministry called Arts Release led some songs. The group prompted us to sing refrains in other languages, led at least one song that flipped between languages, and combined instruments that are rarely heard together. We might expect this kind of approach at a Bible translation conference, but what about in a church? Can something as messy, unexpected, and unfamiliar as multilingual worship work in an ordinary church?

The Problem with English

There are various approaches of how, when, and where to introduce different languages. Many websites and resources offer helpful suggestions, some of which can be found in chapter 16. Yet I think we make a mistake when we run straight to the models and methods without taking stock of what it means to use different languages in our church services. For me, this process began with one annoying realization.

British people are notoriously bad tourists.

One recent newspaper story described a British lady who wrote to her holiday tour company to complain that too many people in her hotel spoke Spanish all the time—she was on holiday in Spain! In parts of continental Europe, there are little islands of Britishness, signs in English, British pubs, British shops selling British chocolate and British food, and even the odd British chip shop. It seems that, wherever Brits go, they like to impose Britishness.

> *Can something as messy, unexpected, and unfamiliar as multilingual worship work in an ordinary church?*

This attitude can easily apply to churches. Brits abroad might look hard for an English-speaking church when on holiday and not give a second thought to the idea that people who use other languages might look for something similar in the UK. Even in churches where other languages are spoken, people often sing translations of songs originally sung in English, to the point where an English-speaker can sing along, even without knowing a word of the local language.

Like it or not, English-language expressions, English-language worship, and even English-language ways of thinking and talking about the Bible have become global. We tend to forget how easily our categories, expectations, and behaviors have been conditioned by our language. In the church world, we forget about the effects of British missionary activity in the nineteenth and early twentieth centuries,[1] followed by present day "US-ian"[2]—and to a lesser extent Australian—worship, preaching, and church leadership.

Multilingual church of any sort runs against wider church trends. True, there are important and valuable indigenous church traditions around the world, but sadly, the rise in social media and the globalization of church worship means that these are often sidelined in a world where countries with technological advantages become influential simply because of those advantages. It is ironic that the same technologies that enable churches to reach a global audience (see chapter 1) also enable a comparatively small segment of Christianity to become a cultural force around the world. I do not claim that this was ever deliberate and I certainly don't assume that those whose voices are most heard are using their influence for nefarious purposes. But English wields considerable power because it is so common online—over 50 percent of all websites are in English.[3]

This power can be easily taken for granted in churches. In one of the earliest books on multiethnic church, Manuel Ortiz gave the following definition: "The multiethnic church includes culturally diverse people who meet together as one congregation, utilizing one language, usually English."[4]

This is not a minority view. With a few exceptions,[5] research on multiethnic church often ignores or minimizes the fact that different languages might exist in the same church or takes the model of different services in different languages as the only way to do multilingual church.[6] Since most such research comes from English-speaking countries, the dominance of English is upheld. In fact, one leader of a multiethnic church specifically wrote the following about multilingual worship:

---

1 Kwiyani, *Multicultural Kingdom*, 8–62.
2 I am deliberately using the rather awkward term "US-ian" here, as the term "American" can, and perhaps should, mean anyone from the American continents. Even "North American" could reasonably be assumed to cover the USA and Canada.
3 W3Techs, "Usage Statistics."
4 Ortiz, *One New People*, 86.
5 For example: Scott and Scott, "Heart-Language Worship"; Han, "Social Inclusion," 383–98; Kouega and Ndzotom, "Multilingual Practices," 45–58; DeYmaz and Li, *Leading a Healthy*.
6 Garces-Foley, *Crossing the Ethnic Divide*, 156–57; Marti, "Fluid Ethnicity"; Gray, *High Definition Leader*.

> It may help to subtly reduce a sense of superiority and allow people to recognise that English is only one of the languages of heaven. The point here is not to undermine English as the usual, dominant language of communication in an English-speaking environment, but equally not to dismiss too quickly the notion of appreciating the diversity of languages known and spoken in a multicultural church.[7]

This short passage illustrates the tension that exists when churches attempt to reflect the linguistic diversity of their members. The tension is especially strong when those churches have accepted the dominance of English. On the one hand, the author makes clear that the dominance of English can create a sense of linguistic superiority—as if English were the best or most spiritual language—and that this superiority must be challenged. Yet on the other hand, he is careful to note that this is not an exercise in challenging the place of English in the church.

Can we ever really challenge linguistic superiority without challenging the dominance of English? Any attempt to have another language spoken or used from the front in church is, whether we realize it or not, a challenge to the dominance and superiority of English. If we have a biblical conviction to become a multilingual church but still want the church services, discipleship, and worship in English or in any locally dominant language then we have a contradiction at best.

By singing songs in other languages, we affirm that these languages are worthy of use in sung worship. Praying in other languages demonstrates that those languages are suitable for talking to God. Giving announcements in other languages tells the congregation that those languages can communicate important information. Preaching in another language demonstrates that God speaks in other languages.

If we find ourselves asking how the English speakers in our church might understand people singing in Farsi, praying in French, or preaching in Fula, then we might want to ask how speakers of other languages will understand while we sing in English, pray in English, and preach in English. The same can be said about any locally dominant language. The discomfort that some scholars have noted among English speakers when hearing people sing in other languages[8] is just a reflection of the discomfort that speakers of minority languages face every day of their lives. We need incarnational thinking that invites speakers of the locally dominant language to experience their language being marginalized.

---

7 Patten, *Leading a Multicultural Church*, 84.
8 Aldous, Dunmore, and Seevaratnam, *Intercultural Church*, 18–19.

How might our thinking change if we experience the need for translation or interpreting? How might we change our expectations if our language was not the one heard or seen from the pulpit or printed in the Bibles? Might dethroning English, or whichever language is dominant, be the key to unlocking people's thinking?

As we think through the experience of having one service that involves several different languages, we must take seriously the possibility that "undermin[ing] English as the usual, dominant language of communication" might be necessary if we are to build truly multilingual churches.[9] After all, no language was dominant on Pentecost, despite the fact that there were plenty of candidates. So why should there be dominant languages in our churches?

Hearing Your Language Spoken

Because of the dominance of English, many of us can take for granted how special it is to hear our language spoken outside our home countries. Malcolm Patten explains:

> It can be liberating and affirming for a person to speak, worship, and pray in a mother tongue when otherwise, if speaking in English, one may have to translate when one speaks and may thus lack fluency. ... Even those present whose own language or culture is not expressed will see that their church is a place where everyone is welcome for who they are and with the languages they speak.[10]

By voluntarily offering space to other languages, we preach a powerful message about how we see languages and how God sees them. By preaching that message, we are also naturally preaching a message of how much we love people and how much God loves them. This immensely practical message gives people the freedom to be who God made them to be and to express themselves fluently in the words or signs that they use habitually.

This message also communicates clearly the identity and nature of the church. It tells people that they are welcome and they will find others who understand their experience. It communicates that the church's values and identity include accepting and affirming different languages

---

9 Research is increasingly showing the importance of undermining the idea of the church having a single dominant language. Research on practices in Catholicism has shown that having regular services with bilingual liturgies, alongside encouraging people to meet together, strongly predicts how well Hispanic people will integrate into parishes in the US. See Reynolds and Reynolds, "The Integration of Hispanic Parishioners" and Starks and Adler "What Veteran Parishes Can Teach Us."

10 Patten, *Leading a Multicultural Church*, 82–83.

and the people who speak or sign them. Any display of another language on stage, whether singing in another language or having interpreting on stage, says that this church values those languages.

Are there limits to the space we can offer other languages? If we accept that each church will have a dominant language, then there must be. It will be refreshing, of course, for someone to walk into our churches and hear someone pray or sing in their language. But that refreshment will be limited since, at some point, the service will revert back to its default language. In short, in churches where one language is dominant, the wonderful visuals of having other languages heard or seen from the front are only signs that a language is accepted, not that it is equal.

To challenge the dominance of certain languages in our churches, we must remove the limits on how and when they can be used. Use of minority languages can be just as common as the dominant language. Written translations and explanations of what is said, sung, or preached mean that people could take part, even if their language is not being used. Interpreting could also be used where written translation is not appropriate or possible. For example, many preachers do not use manuscripts, so the final form of the sermon might be determined as the preacher is speaking. As we will see in the next four chapters, on such occasions, interpreting does even more than simply close any language gaps.

> **To challenge the dominance of certain languages in our churches, we must remove the limits on how and when they can be used.**

In this kind of fully multilingual church, the languages people hear and see from the front are more than just affirmations that different languages exist. They affirm that these languages hold an equal place in the life of the church. They demonstrate that the church accepts temporary discomfort in the process of learning to be a multilingual community together. In such a church, no one group has the monopoly on decision making and no one language is given more importance than any other.

The Identity of a Multilingual Church

Some may argue that this is all well and good but, at some point, a church must put a marker down to establish once and for all who the church is and how it speaks. To some leaders, a church without a dominant language might sound like a recipe for chaotic babble. How on earth could anything get done if anyone can just go around using whichever language they feel like?

Chapters 11 and 12 cover the actual mechanics of offering language provision in churches. What matters more at this point is confronting the assumption that a single, dominant language is the only way to operate. Two perspectives are worth considering: the perspective of leaders, as they look to help people grow into the people God has called them to be, and the perspective of those in the congregation, as they work out what it means to be part of such a church.

The Leadership Perspective

From the perspective of leaders, having a single, dominant language seems logical, but doing so will always shut some people out. It is completely different to preach, lead, teach, or learn in your second or third or fourth language than it is in your first. I am happy to read the Bible, listen to sermons, and even, if I have sufficient time to prepare, preach in French. Yet that level of comfort is the result of two university degrees involving French, an academic year in the country, and being around the language since I was eight. That doesn't even count all the time I have spent listening to, reading, and speaking French. Even with all that training, education, and time, I still preach far more fluently in English than French.

Whether we like it or not, whether it is comfortable or not, as soon as we have areas of church life and service where it is absolutely necessary to speak or sign or even write in the locally dominant language to a high level, we severely limit who can serve there. Put another way, our imposition of a dominant language forces people onto the sidelines and limits their participation.

Excluding people based on their language skills is simply poor leadership. If we believe that God wants everyone in our church serving effectively then we need to work at removing the linguistic barriers that might exclude them.

I say that *we* need to work at removing these barriers because it is surprisingly easy to add to others' burdens by making it their job to remove language barriers. A church can certainly provide language classes, but something has gone wrong when these classes become a prerequisite for serving effectively in the church. Facilitating relationships between people who speak different languages is wonderful. It is not so wonderful to treat ministry to people without the locally dominant language as in some way inferior to or separate from the rest of the church.

It is worth noting that these exclusions aren't just about who can sing, preach, or pray in the big services. Chapter 15 guides us through the different points at which people might come into contact with our church and what kind of language provision might be needed at each point.

Here, it's worth asking the same question about people already in the church. Which ministries or opportunities are inaccessible if you don't speak the locally dominant language? How much can someone actually contribute to your church and how much can they give and receive ministry while still using their first language?

A core part of the identity of multilingual churches is their commitment to remove any barriers that would prevent people from being reached, taught, or discipled, as well as the barriers that might prevent people from serving. Using different languages, on as equal terms as possible, becomes part of what it means to belong to that church (chapter 9). The leaders then make it their business to address places where people might get stuck in the process. When being multilingual becomes part of the identity of the church, people are not required to spend months or years learning the locally dominant language before they can participate fully in the life of the church; the life of the church goes on in many different languages, all at the same time.

This approach enables leaders of multilingual church to fulfill this mandate:

> Now these are the gifts Christ gave to the church: the apostles, the prophets, the evangelists, and the pastors and teachers. Their responsibility is to equip God's people to do his work and build up the church, the body of Christ. This will continue until we all come to such unity in our faith and knowledge of God's Son that we will be mature in the Lord, measuring up to the full and complete standard of Christ. (Eph 4:11–13, NLT)

This passage leads to a very important question: how much does the "equipping" in your church depend on everyone speaking the same language? As long as people need to share a common language to be equipped, the church has parts of the body telling others that their impact on the body is limited (1 Cor 12). From a leadership point of view, having different languages in the same service is more than just symbolism. It is a declaration of intent and a theological claim, marking who the church is and what the church aspires to be.

The Point of View of Those in the Church

From the point of view of those in the church, the above declaration of intent leads to three important realizations. First, as Malcolm Patten reminded us earlier, using different languages on a Sunday makes people feel valued. Imagine walking into a church where your language is not spoken. Now imagine walking into a different church where your language is spoken. Which one would feel more welcoming?

Hearing different languages spoken in church leads to a second realization: this church goes the extra mile. Having different languages in the same service will produce discomfort. It is tricky to get right. Yet being in a church that considers the price worth paying is refreshing, especially to people who are living everyday life in their second or third language. But not everyone is comfortable in multilingual environments—chapter 14 covers the tensions this can create among speakers of the dominant language.

The final realization is that, if someone on the stage is speaking my language, I know that I can serve in that language too. Any language that is validated from the front becomes validated as a language of worship, service, teaching, prayer, and all other aspects of church life. This is why we must avoid segregating languages to specific spaces where they can be used. If we can pray in a language, but the language will never be used in preaching, then we shut out people with preaching gifts who use that language. If we're happy to sing a song in a language or put a translation on the screen but will never allow it in children's ministry or prayer, then we are implicitly telling people that their language is fine as a symbol but not as a full part of church life.

The Questions Posed by Different Languages in the Same Service

Having different languages in the same services poses two sets of questions. The first set consider the practicalities of making different languages work. The second set addresses how churches can be led through the process.

The practical questions include:

- How will people understand what is said or signed in another language?
- Do we need to pre-translate what is said?
- Can we teach songs that have different versions in different languages?
- Should we use interpreting?
- Should we use a pre-written and translated liturgy?
- What does it look and feel like for people to join into worship that isn't in their language?
- Which parts of the service are we ready to have in other languages now? How can we expand this?

- What would it be like for someone to preach in a language that isn't the locally dominant one?
- What about leading worship in another language? What tools and preparation do we need to make this work?

Chapters 11 and 12 cover some possible answers to these questions. Every church has to make their own decisions based on the tools, resources, and people available. Church leaders also need to be aware of where the church is at the moment and how much it can change at one time. As a first step, the church could invite someone to lead a prayer or sing a special song in another language. Progress, even in small steps, really does matter, and an incremental approach helps to ensure that the church doesn't get stuck half-way.

Next, are the leadership questions, which again need to be answered for each church. These questions include:

- How do we prepare people for the productive discomfort that comes from experiencing different languages in the service?
- What values need to be taught, preached, and modeled for this to work?
- What preparatory teaching needs to be covered?
- What might we start to change now?
- What price are we prepared to pay for the cause of reaching, teaching, and discipling people in our community, no matter which language they speak?

I would dearly love to have all the answers laid out. Certainly, Western Christianity loves its categories and answers and how-to guides. I am not sure that hunger for an immediate, clear answer is always biblical, however. Living out the calling to be churches that manifest the multilingual reality of heaven is not something we do by following formulas.

I am a dad of six. I can read all the parenting books I want and take all the parenting courses I can, but in the end, those ideas can only go from examples and principles to real-life action by practice, prayer, and trying things. I have found that I can't even parent any two of my children the same way, as each child has their different strengths, weaknesses, needs, and gifts. If I tried to parent them all the same, it would be a mess.

The same likely holds true for churches. Incorporating other languages in your church will be different from the church across the street and certainly different from the church ten miles away. The look and feel of having different languages in the same service will be unique to each church. For this reason, it is essential to understand all the tools available to help you on your journey.

In the next four chapters, we will look at different approaches that churches can take to using different languages, illustrating these with the example of how different churches approach interpreting. These different approaches to languages have important implications for the success of multilingual church.

CHAPTER 6

Artificial Intelligence to the Rescue?

Learning another language is hard. As I write this, I am trying to motivate myself to consolidate the Finnish I have learned so far, so I can start adding new grammar and vocabulary. My German is shaky and usually wrong, and even in French, my working language, I need to recheck some structures in formal writing every time I write an email. And that is despite having been around the language for the past thirty years.

Imagine if there existed a portable, cheap system that did away with all that and allowed anyone to speak any language at the touch of a button. Is it possible? The makers of speech interpreting apps and devices certainly want us to think so, but is there truth to their claims?

Faced with the seemingly insurmountable problem of reaching, teaching, and discipling communities that speak multiple languages, it is no wonder that churches look for simpler solutions. If churches decide they want everyone together in the same room at the same time, it seems to make sense to grab some kind of interpreting app (often called speech translation or machine interpreting). After all, most of them are free and they allow people to listen to the service in a dizzying array of languages at no cost to the church.

But is everything as perfect as it sounds? Does it make sense to ask machine interpreting or speech translation apps to take care of the service? Where might such apps be useful and where will they likely lead to embarrassment? Before we get into the nitty-gritty of what it is like to rely on speech translation apps, it is important to have a very brief primer on how they work. Knowing how they work provides insight into deciding where to use them.[1]

How Do Speech Translation Apps Work?

There are two main ways to get computers to produce speech translation. The first is called the cascade model and works like this:

- First, the app takes what someone says and turns it into written text. This is called speech recognition.

---

[1] For a more detailed account of how these apps work and what they mean for interpreting, read my earlier book, *Interpreters vs Machines: Can Interpreters Survive in an AI-Dominated World?*

- Next, the app passes this text through a machine translation system that creates text in another language.
- Finally, the text in the other language is passed to a speech synthesis module, which reads that text aloud.
- Do that over and over again for each stretch of speech and you have something that looks like interpreting.

The other way to get computers to produce speech translation is much simpler. Called the "end-to-end model," it involves feeding computers huge amounts of spoken sentences in different languages and getting the computer to predict which sound to generate based on the samples it has in its database. There is no text involved, no machine translation stage, just sound in one language to sound in the other.

Each approach has its advantages and disadvantages. The cascade model uses technologies that have been available for years and are constantly being developed. Speech recognition is getting better all the time and is better able to cope with accents fast speech, and even limited background noise. With a few tweaks, it can even insert punctuation.

Machine translation dates back to the Cold War and the newest techniques in this area show impressive results. It is now possible—if you have the time, technological know-how, and computing power—to train your own machine translation model. This can reduce worries over privacy and make sure that the right terminology is used—such as the right phrase for the Lord's Supper, Communion, or the Eucharist. Speech synthesis still sounds robotic but it is useful enough that I used the speech synthesis capabilities of Microsoft Word to help me edit drafts of this book. With a little tweaking, it is also possible to select a specific computer-generated "voice" for speech synthesis too.

The cascade model does have some serious limitations, though. For a start, it can be relatively slow. Each step takes considerable computing power and, unless you happen to have an app with a fast connection to a powerful server, there may be a noticeable delay. Some apps also are only good enough for a few sentences at a time, not anything close to interpreting an entire church service.

The worst problems of the cascade model come from its nature. The fact that it is essentially based on text means that emotions, intonation, and emphasis all get lost. It also means that the output will mostly be flat and the tone will sound exactly the same if the original speaker says, "I am really pleased to see you" as it will if they say, "I am very sorry for your loss," or "I am very angry."

More dangerously, errors tend to compound quickly. Mishearing in the speech recognition stage means that the wrong text will go to the machine translation model, which will lead to a poor translation being sent to the speech synthesis module. The old computing phrase "garbage in, garbage out" applies here. Since background noise is an issue with speech recognition, even given recent improvements, it is surprisingly easy for the cascade model to go wrong.

The end-to-end model is much newer and seems like it could correct for most of those problems. Going straight from audio to audio with no text stage in the middle seems like it should reduce problems around emotions. But end-to-end models are still very new, and training your own seems all but impossible right now, unless you happen to have hundreds of thousands of samples in each of the languages you need, all perfectly aligned and ready.

This means that end-to-end models can suffer an even worse problem with terminology than cascade models and might not be available for many languages. While they can run faster, systems using the end-to-end model can also sound noticeably choppier between sentences than output from the cascade model. There also seems to be a noticeable lack of free apps using the end-to-end model and the reproduction of emotions still has a long way to go. Background noise can also pose a similar problem as in the cascade model. Garbage in always produces garbage out.

Are They Suitable for Use in Church?

The answer to this question is more complex than you might think. As a trained interpreter, I would dearly love to say that machine interpreting systems should be thrown out the window and never talked about again. But that would be intellectually dishonest.

Machine interpreting has advantages over using humans. It is available in more places, at more times, and in more situations than human interpreters could ever be. It is cheaper than humans, even volunteers, and has provided access to interpreting to more people than ever before. It can also be used to automatically generate subtitles and written translation from speech. But it isn't perfect.

Machine interpreting might be cheaper than humans, but it still comes at a price. Using free apps means that everything you say is used to train the interpreting system. This makes such apps unsuitable for use when there are concerns around privacy or safety.

The lack of emotion in the cascade model and the tendency for machine interpreting to lack vocabulary specific to any church means that using it in sermons is risky and should most likely be avoided. As a simple example, I was recently playing with Microsoft Translate at the invite of people running a Christian conference on intercultural church. At one point, the speaker said, "I don't know what kind of food they were selling" and Microsoft Translate offered the French for "I don't know what devil they were selling" as the translation.

This is aside from any theological concerns. For example, in Google Translate I found that, for written text, it tended to turn Protestant church terms in English into Roman Catholic terms in French. Since the same machine translation system is currently powering the interpreting function of Google Translate, that flaw would exist if it were used in churches.

Machine interpreting also struggles with music or when there is substantial background noise. To make it work consistently, it needs high quality sound directly from a unidirectional microphone at the right distance from the speaker. This is remarkably similar to what human interpreters need, although human interpreters deal much better with background noise.

On the positive side, machine interpreting is highly portable and can be available in several places at once. It can be in the pockets of people welcoming folks as they come in the door, accessible to the parking team and used in the nursery and children's church, all at the same time. It can help several people at the same time during church meals, enabling different conversations to go on at once. Technologies related to machine interpreting can also be used to help human interpreters, by providing live checks on terminology, names, and Scripture verses.

The question therefore is not so much "are machine interpreting apps suitable for use in church?" but, "where can such apps be put to good use?" Their limitations mean that they aren't suitable for replacing humans during the service. We should also ask hard questions about the theology of having a machine re-preach the sermon in another language. Unless we believe that robots can preach the Word of God, should we be entrusting them with interpreting the preaching of the Word of God?

Making Smart Use of Machine Interpreting Apps

Despite their limitations, it would be a mistake to dismiss such apps completely, especially given that the language needs of churches are often much wider and more complex than interpreting sermons. Much more happens in the life of a church than gathering on a Sunday, and machine interpreting can play a part in that wider life of the church. Let's imagine what this might look like.

Artificial Intelligence to the Rescue?

A visitor from another country arrives in the church for the first time. On the door, someone quickly realizes that they do not speak the language of the church and so pulls out an interpreting app. The app quickly detects both languages and allows the welcomer to briefly introduce themselves and welcome the visitor to the church.

Inside, clear signage instructs the visitor how to download the same app the welcomer used, which can translate text as well as speech. The ushers again use their own devices to make the visitor feel welcome and point out that interpreting is available, from trained humans, throughout the service.

If the visitor has children, they can be taken to children's church, where all the leaders and volunteers know which language the children speak and use their apps to welcome the children and explain some basic details about children's church, while trained interpreters help during the lesson itself.

> **We cannot expect machine interpreting apps to instantly solve all communication problems.**

After the service, the regular members of the church are already adept in having conversations using the app. As a result, within a few minutes, the visitor is invited to a small group where their language is spoken, while their children make new friends.

Pulling Apart the Example

The above example might seem more than a little idealistic. After all, sometimes it is hard enough to get people used to saying hello to visitors. Expecting an entire church to get used to pulling out an interpreting app seems as if it would require superhuman feats of persuasion and training.

The example above probably does represent the absolute best case. It does, however, point to some key considerations. The first and most important is that machine interpreting works best when it is part of a coherent and well thought-out strategy. Given its strengths and weaknesses, this means that machine interpreting will work best when paired with other ways of providing for people's language needs.

A coherent machine interpreting strategy must therefore be part of a wider language provision strategy (chapter 11) and its implementation (chapter 12). We cannot expect machine interpreting apps to instantly solve all communication problems. Instead, they need to be integrated with human translation and interpreting, multilingual signage, and distribution of resources across all parts and ministries of the church. This approach will help to build and maintain a church where linguistic and cultural diversity is at the heart of the church's identity and values.

A second consideration is that successful machine interpreting roll-out relies on having the technology to provide it and the expertise to use it well. In most cases, this will likely mean that the longer-term goal would be for the church to combine machine and human interpreting and machine translation onto a single app. It also means that a church can find itself in a position where a bank of suitable devices is made freely available to anyone who needs them. People who have recently fled persecution are unlikely to arrive at the door of the church sporting the latest smart phone. If machine interpreting is to break down barriers and not create new ones, any church using it for more than a single language will need to be proactive in making sure that those who need it have the technological means to access it.

For a single language, it might be tempting to have just a small number of interpreting devices, used by a select set of volunteers and perhaps broadcasting to a small number of headsets. The problem with this is that it takes power away from those coming into the church, turning the church into the beneficent donor of language access while visitors become the grateful, but ultimately powerless, recipients. Switching away from people having access to their own devices can also limit their ability to chat with people outside of formal church services. This limits how well speakers of other languages can integrate into the church. Conversely, having a small number of devices can be much easier to manage and discourages people from being on their phones throughout the service.

One final consideration, which I have tried to represent in the example, is that machine interpreting provision really needs to be coupled with clear communication about how and when to use it. Finding ways to let people know that they can get access to an app, either on their own device or on devices that they can borrow from the church, is vital. This gives people the ability to have some power over their own interpreting decisions, by allowing them to start conversations themselves or even to choose to go without the app at all.

Using machine interpreting devices requires discipline. In a normal, monolingual conversation, people interrupt each other, speak over each other, leave sentences unfinished, and use all sorts of ways to signal that they are still listening. Machine interpreting devices and apps work best when people are disciplined enough to not interrupt and have clear turns. This makes the conversation stilted and so these devices are not at all a replacement for human interpreters, who learn how to manage conversations.

Such apps also cannot replace language learning. Language learning is not simply something that churches should expect people from other countries to do but should be common across everyone in the church. It says a lot when someone who speaks the locally dominant language chooses to learn the languages of those who come to the church from around the world.

If anything, the care that needs to be taken when using machine interpreting should make us more aware of just how important it is to be ready to learn someone else's language. Machine interpreting devices can play an important role in churches but they are certainly not a perfect cure. In fact, not even human interpreting can work on its own, unless it is properly integrated into the church. In the next chapter, we will find out why.

CHAPTER 7

Interpreting in the Corner

This time, I was literally in a corner. Our church was meeting in the prayer room, while we were waiting for building work on the main sanctuary to be completed. The room was already what you might charitably call "cozy." I sat in a corner of that small room, surrounded by a handful of people from the Democratic Republic of Congo. From the moment the pastor started preaching, I leaned over and whispered my French version into the ears of those around me. It wasn't comfortable for anyone.

As it was a typical charismatic church, sermons involved a decent amount of volume changes. Since I was whispering, I couldn't change the volume of my voice. Those listening to me had to lean in further if the preaching got louder. Of course, I had to lean over too. I am sure I must have had to stretch a few times, forcing my audience to move their heads to catch what I was saying.

It was uncomfortable for those who didn't need the interpreting too. Sure, no one expected the church to be silent during the sermon but it takes a special interpreter to ignore stares or requests to quieten down. Although the interpreting was in the corner, it affected everyone in the church.

In a sense, it was a blessing that it didn't last very long. After a few weeks, the number of people who needed interpreting dwindled to zero as they missed the minibus the church put on for them. After a rather uncomfortable interpreted meeting explaining how the church leadership were frustrated at the time being lost sending a minibus to get people who didn't arrive, the church soon went back to being monolingual.

The interpreting lasted exactly as long as our visitors kept coming. It started due to a need and disappeared when the need was gone. The identity and mission of the church never needed interpreting or any language but English. The corner where I used to whisper was taken up with people who only spoke English, as if nothing out of the ordinary had ever happened.

Signs the Interpreting Is an Accident

When churches face language barriers, what happens next is often made up on the spot. If people realize that something is needed but there aren't enough people to have a full service in another language, some kind of interpreting will often take place. This could mean using a machine interpreting app (chapter 6) or finding volunteers from the church. The interpreting isn't something the church intended to do. It just finds itself doing it to meet an immediate need. The interpreting is accidental.

> **When churches face language barriers, what happens next is often made up on the spot.**

Accidental interpreting, also called incidental interpreting,[1] seems to be the most common approach in churches and in the commercial world. There is nothing inherently wrong with this approach. It is much better to provide some kind of interpreting than none at all and, with a few exceptions (chapter 8), most of the interpreting that becomes excellent starts out accidental.

There are clear signs that interpreting is accidental. One of the most obvious is that people expect it to be invisible. For her master's thesis, experienced church interpreter, Irina Peremota,[2] surveyed 146 churches in twenty-four countries and found that it was common for them to emphasize the interpreter's professional skills and their ability to make themselves invisible and blend into the background. This was more common than any requirements for the interpreters to be Christians.

This desire for the interpreting to become invisible marks it out as something the church needs but doesn't really want. In accidental interpreting, people talk about interpreters as conduits or pipes or invisible or the voice of the speaker. Who the interpreter is becomes much less important than their ability to just say what the speaker said and do so as unobtrusively as possible.

One of the two churches I studied for my PhD saw interpreting as incidental. From the stage, one leader lamented the fact that a national leader had to interpret for visiting speakers when they visited his church.[3] Another leader told me that the interpreter was "only a channel"[4] and wasn't free to make any of their own decisions. Interpreting in that church only existed when there was a genuine and unavoidable language need. As soon as people got good enough at English, the interpreting at meetings disappeared. If no volunteers could be found, people would just be expected to muddle along.

---

1 Downie, "Stakeholder Expectations," 169.
2 Peremota, "Church Interpreting," 3, 44, 48.
3 Downie, "Stakeholder Expectations," 133.
4 Downie, 135.

Accidental interpreting is often temporary interpreting. It is certainly interpreting with no explicit commitment or strategy. What might this look like on a typical Sunday? Some of the following is likely to happen:

- Most people in the church are unaware the interpreting exists.
- There is no actual rota or schedule for the interpreting. People are just asked on the day or it is assumed they will do the job if they arrive.
- The interpreters don't receive any notes in advance and have to muddle through.
- The interpreting equipment, if it exists, is poorly maintained and the audio-visual team might forget to switch it on or only check to confirm it works when the service has already started.
- Those speaking or signing on the stage forget the interpreting exists and so routinely speak or sign too quickly or make lots of jokes or statements that only make sense if you are a user of the locally dominant language.
- If the interpreter is on stage next to the speaker, they are often interrupted, or the speaker goes on too long before pausing.
- There is no pastoral support for interpreters and so they can work in highly emotional meetings or interpret traumatic testimonies without anyone checking on them afterwards.
- There are frequent reports of discouragement and burnout among the interpreters.
- Church leaders are considering replacing the interpreters with artificial intelligence or asking people to bring their phones to use interpreting apps.

It must be said that accidental interpreting can work and, for many churches, it is the route towards providing interpreting of any form. Accidental interpreting does provide a viable way for churches to meet the needs of people who speak different languages. It might start with finding a willing volunteer who knows how to whisper or how to hold a microphone and could lead to the church buying in expensive equipment or professional interpreting later on, as their approach changes.

Accidental interpreting is not defined by the cost of the equipment but the connection between the interpreting and the rest of the church. This connection determines how consistent the interpreting will be, how much of an impact it will have, and what it will feel like to be an interpreter or an interpreting user. Interpreting that muddles along without a plan tends to flounder and eventually disappear. Interpreting that is part of a wider strategy will make a lasting difference. This pattern doesn't just apply to interpreting. It works for any kind of multilingual church. While researching this book, I came across an article by Brian Starks and Gary J. Adler Jr that for Catholic parishes in the USA to integrate both Hispanic and English-speaking people into the church, regular bilingual masses were needed.[5] Being multilingual only seems to work if it is a vital part of church life. Since finding and keeping people with language skills is necessary for any church that is looking to offer any language provision, it is worth examining what it feels like to be an accidental interpreter. This experience will be familiar to anyone providing accidental language services.

What Accidental Interpreting Feels Like

There is no better place to understand what accidental interpreting feels like than in the research of Finnish interpreter and interpreting trainer, Sari Hokkanen. She spent years cataloging and analyzing her experience as an interpreter in two different Pentecostal churches and at a Lutheran church conference in Finland. Here, she describes the working conditions at that conference:

> This was a family service, so the arena was full and there were a lot of children. Luckily, not many people came to sit right next to me. I still had to constantly monitor my surroundings, and once I turned to ask for a family with three small kids to maybe try to keep it a little quieter. I tried to do it as politely as I could, because I don't think the people around me realized what I was doing there. I spoke in English into this small microphone taped to my cheek, but otherwise there wasn't anything that separated me from a normal attendant, by appearances at least. This being the third day of interpreting in less than perfect conditions, my voice seemed to be a little strained, but otherwise the interpreting went fine. Somehow it all felt external to me, though. All the phrases and the vocabulary were familiar, but it didn't feel the same as interpreting at my home church.[6]

In this account, there are several signs that point to the limitations and risks of accidental interpreting. If I were to show this to my professional colleagues, they would start worrying about the lack of suitable equipment. Here is an interpreter without a soundproof booth, without

---

5 Starks and Adler, "What Veteran Parishes Can Teach Us," 495.
6 Hokkanen, "Experiencing the Interpreter's Role," 62–78.

a movable microphone and without any shielding from the noise around them. It makes sense therefore that her voice is becoming strained. She is having to balance interpreting and keeping those around her quiet. The interpreter seems detached from what is going on. These just aren't sustainable conditions.

Show this excerpt to an experienced church interpreter and they will spot those things and might add an additional problem: no one is aware that this person is interpreting. For those nearby, it would have seemed that some random person is constantly talking through the entire service while telling the people around them to be quiet! This is not going to go down well and will create tension between the interpreter and the congregation.

Accidental interpreting puts interpreters in tricky situations. It leaves them with the difficult task of negotiating how and where they will work and trying to find a place, any place, where they can deliver the interpreting people need. This puts more pressure on them and increases the stress that comes with interpreting.

Accidental interpreting puts the people who need interpreting into tricky situations too. It places the onus on those who need the interpreting to go and find it, provide feedback to the interpreter, and muddle through if things go wrong. It also leaves those people stranded if the interpreter can't make it or if for some reason, the interpreting doesn't work.

Finally, accidental interpreting puts those who don't need the interpreting in very tricky situations. Imagine having to put up with someone interrupting the preacher every sentence or muttering incessantly throughout the service! Imagine trying to enjoy the service when the person near you won't stop whispering to this group of people you don't even know. Even if people partially understand the idea that interpreting is there, it will soon seem like an unnecessary burden or discomfort.

Yet accidental interpreting does work, to the point that some people will understand more than they could without it. It is an important stepping stone. Yet it comes with serious flaws. It feels uncomfortable for the interpreter. It creates tension between the interpreter and those around them. It makes it more likely that people will resent the presence of interpreting and, by extension, the presence of the people who need it.

While researchers have shown just how well church interpreters can do their job, even under less-than-ideal conditions,[7] working under such

---

7 da Silva, Soares, and Esqueda, "Interpreting in a Religious"; Tan, Amini, and Lee, "Challenges Faced by Non-Professional," 53–74.

conditions constantly can have long-term mental and physical effects. For example, working with unsuitable equipment can permanently damage interpreters' hearing.[8] This could be due to a one-time shock from a sudden noise[9] or longer-term tinnitus and discomfort due to ongoing poor-quality sound.

Churches can also underestimate the emotional and mental toll that interpreting can take. When interpreters relay an emotional testimony, they can often feel those emotions too.[10] When the sermon is dealing with some complex theological point, the interpreters need to unravel it too, in real-time. Interpreting is hard mental work. What happens in accidental interpreting is that this hard mental work is done quietly and is ignored by everyone else. The hard work of whispering the interpreting through one service is followed by another and another and another, with no help or recognition. The challenge of interpreting next to the preacher is simply followed up by the same thing again but with people starting to get fidgety about why the sermon is taking so long.

It is easy to say that, since interpreting is service to God,[11] the interpreters shouldn't need to be thanked or seen. The act of serving God is its own reward, right? It is true that anyone who serves God for applause or acclaim could do with reading the book of Jeremiah or remembering that the call to follow God is a call to self-denial. Yet, churches are realizing that their leaders need support, resources, prayer, and space. No responsible church would throw a leader into any other ministry without help or resources. We have all seen too many leaders burn out, drop out, or fall to sin. The Bible itself reminds us that,

> Elders who do their work well should be respected and paid well, especially those who work hard at both preaching and teaching. For the Scripture says, "You must not muzzle an ox to keep it from eating as it treads out the grain." And in another place, "Those who work deserve their pay!" (1 Tim 5:17–18, NLT)

It is true that interpreters may or may not be elders but their work is indeed a form of preaching and teaching. To interpret is to re-preach and re-teach: to find the words, signs, intonation, and gestures to represent what was said or signed by someone else. Not every church can afford to pay interpreters, but every church can find ways to support them.

---

8   Reynolds, "Parliamentary Hearings."
9   Harris, "Parliament Hill Interpreter," 27.
10 Tekgül, "Faith-Related Interpreting," 43–57.
11 Hokkanen, "Simultaneous Church Interpreting," 291–309.

Accidental interpreting most often feels like working without support. When it happens, interpreters are often left without help, without useful feedback, and without any idea as to what happens to their work. They are invisible. Since the interpreters and their work are invisible, they are more likely to conclude that their work isn't necessary and to stop serving. If they still continue serving, they are likely to face problems with motivation. The detachment that Sari Hokkanen described in the excerpt above can easily reduce the effectiveness of the interpreting, much as a pastor who stops being connected to God and to their flock ceases to be an effective pastor.

What Can We Do with Accidental Interpreting?

This is all well and good but what can we actually do about accidental interpreting? Is it all doom and gloom—a ministry destined to end in frustration? Not at all. Accidental interpreting is far from ideal, but it can be a stepping stone. Refusing to stop at accidental interpreting can lead us to the point where language services become integral parts of church life. Chapter 9 will discuss what that looks like.

> **Accidental interpreting is far from ideal, but it can be a stepping stone.**

For now, however, it is important to think through what we can do with the accidental interpreting we already have. Not every church is ready to commit to the wholesale changes that it takes to fully integrate interpreting into their work. This often has as much to do with financial constraints as it does with good intentions. Not every church can afford a fancy remote interpreting platform or even soundproof booths. Not every church is ready to have high-quality interpreting from the stage. Is there a way to make the best of what we have?

Absolutely! There are many things that churches can do, even with less-than-ideal accidental interpreting.

The most obvious starting point is to openly acknowledge that the interpreting exists and that it is helpful. Making a point of publicly mentioning that interpreting is available and explaining why it is available shows the church that those people whispering in the corner are doing something meaningful and not just being rude. The same goes for interpreters on stage. While it will always be a bit awkward to interpret a speaker thanking the person who is interpreting for them, small statements explaining why the interpreter is there make the interpreting, and therefore the people who need it, much more visible. Interpreting that is acknowledged and visible is interpreting that soon becomes valued.

Publicly mentioning the interpreting also naturally leads to creating conditions for the interpreting to work better. Providing sermon notes and a rough order of service at least a day in advance allows even untrained volunteers to prepare Scripture references and work out how to deal with any difficult stories. Creating comfortable spaces with excellent audio and visual quality for the interpreters or ensuring that the preacher pauses every sentence or two for the interpreter to speak doesn't just show respect but markedly reduces the stress on the interpreters. Creating mutual feedback mechanisms where interpreters feel comfortable suggesting ways to make the service easier to interpret and where people can offer feedback to the interpreters about their work means that everyone can grow together.

Just because the interpreting started without a plan, that doesn't mean it has to continue without help. Not every church will be comfortable rethinking its entire vision and mission to put languages at their core. But every church can take small steps to offer greater support for those providing language services and can make this work more visible.

Visibility is often a vital factor for the success of language services. Where language services are invisible, they tend to be forgotten, taken for granted and to eventually dwindle to nothing. Invisible interpreting leads to interpreters struggling to find space to work, congregations struggling to understand why the interpreting exists, and churches struggling to justify the continued hard work it takes to keep it going.

An Example from Outside of Church Life

A fairly simple example of this principle can be found in a practical project I had the honor to be part of. In 2018–2019, I was one of a team of four people who supported newly qualified sign language interpreters during their internships with the police and with the National Health Service (NHS) in Scotland, as part of the Promoting Equal Access to Services (PEAS) project. The project had two aims. The first was to help interpreters finishing their training transition to working as professionals. The second, and more relevant aim for this book, was to find ways of better integrating interpreting into the NHS and police.[12]

The police grabbed the opportunity for all it was worth. They arranged familiarization visits to police stations, courts, and prisons, put the word out around police stations in the area, and arranged opportunities for the interpreters to work at real public safety events and on other

---

12 Downie and Turner, "Integrating Interpreting," 235–52.

occasions where there were no direct legal consequences of their work. The police made the project very visible. The results were visible too: officers became more familiar with how to work effectively with interpreters and the interns became more confident in working with the police. In fact, even Deaf prisoners benefitted as the interpreters had the opportunity to point out that the rooms where they received visits from their lawyers were inappropriate as their transparent walls allowed anyone passing by to see what was being signed.

In the NHS, the story was quite different. The interns mostly worked at internal staff meetings, including their own inductions. While they were shown around hospitals, they had little contact with frontline staff. Few people knew the interns were even there and the project had little impact in the organization. The project was mostly invisible and the interns felt that much of their time was wasted.

What does this mean for churches? If interpreting is going to make a positive difference in your church, it will take effort. Interpreting may begin accidentally, but invisible interpreting is ineffective interpreting. Taking small steps, like offering notes, providing space, and making it clear that interpreting is important to your church will make a big difference to how long the interpreting lasts and how long people from other countries stick around in your church.

> **Invisible interpreting is ineffective interpreting.**

CHAPTER 8

We Have a Vision for Languages— One Day We'll Need Them

I thought I knew how this worked. You train as an interpreter, then you graduate, then you market your services, then you get work. Simple, right? Not so much. I trained, I graduated, I wrote to potential clients, especially church clients, and what was the result? Some letters that were never answered and a few that wished me well but told me politely but firmly that there were zero opportunities with this organization, church, or ministry. In fact, one time my wife and I applied to two different missions agencies. One was keen to sign me up but had no idea what to do with my wife. The other was keen to sign up my wife but had no idea what to do with me. So we ended up with neither.

It might sound a bit naïve to say that I thought that being qualified and doing a bit of marketing would instantly lead to full-time interpreting. But that isn't far off how some churches approach the whole issue of being multilingual. While I am convinced that, for the most part, churches end up being multilingual due to some combination of having to deal with people who speak different languages and being planted in a multilingual community, that isn't always the story.

Sometimes churches start out with a vision to be multilingual, even before they actually need to be. And, just like Korie Little Edwards points out regarding multiracial churches,[1] the vision often doesn't match reality. Churches can dream of being multilingual but in reality, they end up being a monolingual church with another language or two used in places. The church is led, the gospel is preached, and the announcements are given in whatever the church language might be. There might be some interpreting somewhere or some words or prayers projected onto a screen in another language but no one really needs it anyway.

> **A vision is not a guarantee of success.**

Just like with chapter 7, I am not writing this to condemn or put down churches who find themselves in this situation. Multilingual church must start somewhere and starting with a vision is better than starting out with a need that the church was never built to fulfill. But a vision is not

---
1 Edwards, "Multiethnic Church Movement."

a guarantee of success. Something else has to happen for a church to become multilingual. To find out what that something else is, it's time to turn to another real-life case study.

When Interpreting Means More than Words

Of all the articles I have read on interpreting in church, one affected me more deeply than any other. Cécile Vigouroux started off with a rather interesting problem. She observed services at Glory Gospel Church, in Cape Town, South Africa. This church stood out for two reasons: first, all the members were Congolese migrants, even though the church was in South Africa,[2] and second, the church offered interpreting of all its sermons into English, even though everyone in the church spoke French and Lingala.[3] What's more, this interpreting was performed in such a way that, for those who didn't speak French, it made little sense. The interpreter often answered the preacher instead of interpreting,[4] skipped segments they did not hear properly or understand,[5] or worked as a partner in a kind of on-stage skit.[6]

When we read about this kind of behavior, we face two main choices, aside from just ignoring it. The first choice is to write it off as bad interpreting. In fact, there are articles on church interpreting where we can find researchers accusing interpreters of acting unprofessionally whenever they step out of what the researchers think they should have done.[7] The other option is to try to figure out why the interpreter acted that way and to understand how that interpreting fits into the church. After all, if someone has been chosen to interpret, the church must have some reason to think they are good enough to do it.

Cécile Vigouroux took the second choice. She interviewed the pastor of the church to understand why the interpreting existed. The answers help us understand what can happen when vision and reality don't meet.

There were two reasons why this admittedly unusual interpreting happened the way it did. The first is that the church had a vision to become a pan-African, French-speaking church.[8] The interpreting was one

---

2 Vigouroux, "Double-Mouthed Discourse," 341.
3 Vigouroux, 342.
4 Vigouroux, 352.
5 Vigouroux, 357–58.
6 Vigouroux, 362–63.
7 Makha and Phafoli, "Distortion of Meaning," 152–63; Musyoka and Karanja, "Problems of Interpreting," 196–207.
8 Vigouroux, "Double-Mouthed Discourse," 345.

of the ways that the church demonstrated its vision, alongside the choice to preach in French and not Lingala. Yet, if the church wanted to be a pan-African, French-speaking church, why would interpreting be provided into English? The church was aware of its precarious position as a migrant church in South Africa, in which none of South Africa's national languages were spoken. The use of English in the service meant that the church had more credibility in its attempts to convince the local Pentecostal Board of its legitimacy.[9]

The interpreting in Glory Gospel Church was therefore not primarily for the people within the church but for the people the church aimed to reach. It also existed for people from other churches who might decide to check on the church to verify that it was acceptable. This interpreting was therefore a kind of performance.

The Importance of Performance

Christians, especially church leaders, are often uncomfortable with the idea of "performance." We often assume that it means something artificial, put on, or false. Anyone familiar with social media or with books on preaching will be familiar with appeals for church to drop "performance"—often connected to flashing lights, smoke, and a noisy sound system—in favor of "real worship" or "authenticity."

That view of performance is short-sighted. Yes, we serve a God who delighted to show up in humble circumstances like a manger. Yes, God warned us of the dangers of spirituality that was just about appearances and not about the heart. But equally, Jesus borrowed a boat from Peter and had it pushed out from shore, so people could hear him better and so he wouldn't be crushed by the crowd (Luke 5:3). Jesus prayed with a loud voice in the temple at least once (John 12:28) and at Lazarus's tomb (John 11). In both cases, Jesus used the resources around him to make sure he was heard and seen better and used his voice to make a point. He could just as well have spoken softly at the tomb or ordered the crowd to go back. Yet, on the shores of Galilee, he used Peter's boat as an impromptu stage and at Lazarus' tomb, he changed his volume from his prayer to his declaration so all the crowd can hear.

Jesus knew the power of public action, especially actions with clear meaning, such as breaking bread (Matt 14:19), making mud with his saliva (John 9:6), and even baptism (Matt 3:13–17). That these actions meant something beyond just pulling bread apart, playing in the dirt, or getting

---

9 Vigouroux, 349.

a body wet is beyond doubt. We might be slightly uncomfortable with labelling them performance.

Yet, if we are to understand the relevance of what happened to Glory Gospel Church, all such actions done to make a point are important. This means that we need a new definition of performance. For our purposes, we will say that performance is any act done in front of an audience, which means more than simply the physical movements it involves and during which the performer is conscious that what they are doing is somehow separate from the rest of their everyday life.[10]

Brushing your teeth in front of your children can be performance, if you are conscious that you are doing it with the implied meaning that they should copy you. A wedding is a performance. A church service is certainly a performance and it can contain all sorts of performative elements, from bowing our heads to pray, to kneeling, raising hands, saying "amen," giving offerings, call and response, laying hands on people, taking communion, and even choosing to preach from a raised pulpit or from a music stand near the congregation. Accepting these things as performances recognizes that what we do has meaning beyond the simple mechanical fact of doing an action.

Of course, we might want to tag on that these actions have to be an echo of what is going on inside us. Religious actions without love for God and dedication to God are condemned several times in the Bible (e.g., Isa 29:13; Hos 6:6; Matt 23:1–24). This does not in any way take away from the fact that we often do actions that reflect some broader meaning. We perform.

Interpreting in Glory Gospel Church was definitely a kind of performance. It might not have worked as a standalone service for people who only spoke English but it demonstrated or performed the fact that the church was open to English speakers. It also performed the vision of the church, to reach across Africa and attract people from different countries. Whether it was technically effective for either of those purposes is a completely different question. The reasons it existed were entirely about performance.

Performing Being a Multilingual Church without Actually Being One

Performance can happen whenever a church wants to have a multilingual congregation but doesn't yet. This can include when a church has a vision for the day when it will need interpreting, or language schools, or

---

10 This definition is closely related to the definitions found in Marvin Carlson's *Performance: A Critical Introduction*.

services, or home groups in different languages. The church prints signs saying "Welcome" in twenty languages. The church buys flags and places them at the front of the church. The church pays for interpreting, invites preachers from around the world, or starts a live stream with subtitles.

It doesn't matter what exactly the church decides to do to tell the world that it is multilingual. Until these services are needed and until there are people who will know quickly if they are not working well, what you have is a symbol of where the church wants to go, not a sign of where it is now.

Remember, there is nothing intrinsically wrong with performance. To some extent, to be human is to perform. Performance becomes a problem when it becomes a replacement for reality, when the fact that something is performed means that people no longer hunger for it to become real.

There is nothing wrong with having interpreting that no one needs right now but, if no one makes an effort to attract people who might need it, and if no one checks to ensure that it would be effective if someone did need it, then there is a problem. There is no issue with having a multilingual welcome sign, but if it takes the place of really welcoming people who speak different languages, then something is wrong.

> *Allowing the dream to be more attractive than the hard work needed to make it reality is dangerous.*

When Words Need to Become Action

It is obvious that the specific pressures on Glory Gospel Church mean that not every church will find itself in a similar situation. What is surprisingly common, however, is that the vision of a church doesn't match up with the reality in which it finds itself or even with the way things currently work. As Korie Little Edwards pointed out in the article I mentioned earlier, it is one thing to start with a great vision of being a diverse church but, if this isn't founded on the commitment to making the changes the vision requires, then the vision is nothing but a nice dream. Allowing the dream to be more attractive than the hard work needed to make it reality is dangerous.

The performative or symbolic side of multilingual church is incredibly powerful. It makes sense to demonstrate to people in our words, actions, and use of space that we value the diversity of languages that God put on the earth. The message that God speaks everyone's language needs to be taught, shown, and known. But, if we only ever get to the showing and miss the hard part of doing what it takes to reach people who speak different languages, listen to their needs, and build multilingual leadership teams, then we are only deceiving ourselves and others.

As much as I love interpreting and as much as I love multilingual worship, the reality is that it is probably responsible to think of those as later stages in the journey. A church has to use the God-given gifts of the people it has to discover the needs of those in its community. It needs to meet the people in their community where they are, find out what language services would help, and then deliver these services in a manageable, sustainable, God-honoring way.

I am all for interpreted or multilingual church meetings, but they are part of the picture, not the entire thing. I once interpreted for a church that decided to run a service interpreted into French but did so on such short notice that they didn't have time to have French Bibles or discipleship resources available for those who came to Christ. This is a minor oversight but one that illustrates the importance of the small details in our work to reach, teach, and disciple our multilingual communities.

Having a vision for languages is definitely a good thing. Let nothing in this chapter discourage you from having such a vision. But for a church to be sustainably multilingual in a way that makes a difference requires both vision and action. Where this combination of vision and action leads is the subject of the next chapter.

CHAPTER 9

Languages Are Who We Are

Facing the Impossible

By this far through the book, multilingual church might seem like an important but impossible dream. If having church only in your locally dominant language is problematic when our communities are multilingual then something must be done. Yet, having services in different languages is fraught with complications and leads to the creation of several churches, not one new multilingual one. Meanwhile, adding several languages into the same service is a powerful symbol but requires real skill and patience to manage well. Relying on machine interpreting is a risky business and having interpreting off in the corner somewhere isn't sustainable. Is there actually a way to do multilingual church well?

The Bible, research, and experience all lead to the same conclusion: multilingual church is God's idea, and it is impossible without him. Looking for models that make things less challenging or that distance us from the difficulties is not a real solution. So many models of multilingual church fall flat because they miss that point.

The biblical call to multilingualism is not a call to build a new ministry or a new group. Neither is it a call to adopt some new technology or to subscribe to some new platform. It is a call to be a new kind of church.

The Gospel Is about Reconciliation

The early church faced a similar and seemingly impossible need for unity over the issue of Jew/Gentile relations in the church in the book of Acts. While the Gentiles were being saved in small numbers and far-off places, things were just about manageable. When God was calling church leaders to eat with Gentiles and when cultural and linguistic conflicts were affecting the church's food program, things became even more tense. Even more acutely, Paul tells us in Galatians 2 that Peter stopped eating with the Gentiles because "he was afraid of criticism from these people who insisted on the necessity of circumcision" (Gal 2:12b, NLT). This, says Paul, is a clear case of "not following the truth of the gospel message" (Gal 2:14a, NLT).

> **Multilingual church is God's idea, and it is impossible without him.**

For Paul, part of the nature of the gospel was that it nullified the split between Jew and Gentile (Eph 2:14). For the gospel to be the gospel and for the church to be the church, there could be no place for any cultural, linguistic, or genetic difference to become a dividing line. The church had to be a place where Jew, Gentile, slave, free, male, and female all lived and ate and grew in discipleship together. Otherwise, it was no longer the church. More to the point, the case of the Galatian church hammers home that this was not some theory about the global church but a necessary reality of local churches. Paul does not want any local church to reflect the divisions, boundaries, and hierarchies of the world around it, any more than it should conform to the restrictions of Jewish laws.

> **We have left behind the paradigm of being here to help the poor internationals. ...**
>
> **Instead, we tell them they are needed as only they can fulfill the international vision.**

The kind of church Paul preached and the kind of church God started building on Pentecost was a multilingual, multiracial, multigenerational, multicultural church that could only be sustained by the grace of God and the power of the Holy Spirit. This is why earthly systems of homogenous units, neatly contained church meetings in different languages, and quiet interpreting that is confined to its own corner are never going to be enough. Something much deeper, much more dangerous, and much more powerful is needed. For that, a trip to Germany is in order.

The Inside-Out Vision

On the first evening of my research visit to Centrum Lebendiges Wort (CLW) in Bonn, Germany, I found myself eating with their senior pastor, Pastor Mario Wahnschaffe, and their international pastor, Pastor Daniel Ondieki. An almost throwaway remark from Pastor Mario ended up framing the entire trip and became a cornerstone of my PhD. He said,

> We have left behind the paradigm of being here to help the poor internationals. ... Instead, we tell them they are needed as only they can fulfill the international vision.[1]

This describes the change in thinking that every church needs to have if it is to become truly, biblically multilingual. There are three stages to this process. The first stage is what I would like to call decentering. To decenter, the church must stop believing that it is here to provide some necessary service to unfortunate migrants. Decentering rejects the

---

1 Downie, "Stakeholder Expectations," 141.

idea that the migrants are in need of help and the church is the savior. In Pastor Mario's words, decentering is "leaving behind the paradigm of being here to help the poor internationals."

Before decentering, the church's image of being multilingual hinges on a clear power imbalance. The locals have the money, the resources, and the decision-making power; the migrants have nothing much to offer. The users of the locally dominant language receive the undiluted, full experience of worship, preaching, and fellowship. The migrants or users of less dominant languages receive whatever the church deigns to offer them. Some folk eat the best of the bread and then create some crumb of language services to ensure that others get fed something.

I do not think that this is ever the intention of any church. Yet, when we tell speakers of other languages that they need to try to pick out information in a language they do not speak, or relegate them to separate services in their own languages, or decide that some software will suffice, we create an imbalance of power and status. These imbalances tell the same story as Peter refusing to eat with Gentiles or some Jewish-background Christians demanding that male converts be circumcised. We would all be shocked at someone claiming Christians should be circumcised or that Christians of different background shouldn't eat together. Yet, before decentering, we unwittingly set up two tables: one for speakers of the dominant language and one for everyone else.

When a church decenters, it looks at itself with honesty and clarity. It asks hard questions about who holds the power, whose interests come first, and which sacrifices are acceptable. A decentered church not only creates some space for speakers of different languages but views multilingualism as a core part of its identity. This means that providing language services is no longer optional but a core part of what it means for the church to exist.

In this sense, a decentered church shares much in common with the church mentioned in chapter 8. Both have a vision to reach, teach, and disciple people from different backgrounds. So what makes the kind of church mentioned in chapter 8 so different from the decentered church we are discussing in this chapter?

Helping People Feel Valued and Needed

Consider the second part of Pastor Mario's quote above. After leaving behind the paradigm of being there to "help the poor internationals," Pastor Mario said that the church assures internationals that "they are needed." Recognizing that we need and value those from other countries is the second stage of decentering and the first concrete move towards building biblical multilingual church. Doing so enables us to notice and address power imbalances and the kinds of decisions that make people feel unwanted and drives them away.

By telling people they are needed, we do more than just use nice words. Telling people they are needed but expecting them to carry the full weight of figuring out how to communicate, worship, listen, and grow in a language they don't understand is, at best, a contradiction. Words are meaningless when they are spoken in a language one cannot understand. When people are able to participate in the life of the church in *their* language, they will be more ready to agree with the idea that they are needed.

Let me give you a very simple monolingual example. My wife and I had been looking to move to Edinburgh for around two years, after the church we used to attend folded. I was travelling about ninety minutes each way to university several days a week to do my PhD and it just made sense to move to Edinburgh. We started looking for churches there for a long time before we managed to move.

We had heard about one particular church, Barnton Baptist Church (now City Gates Baptist Church) beforehand and decided to give it a try. I think that we must have visited about five times in the two years during which we were trying to move. Every time we visited, someone in the church offered to allow us to stay overnight, so we could make the morning service. Most of the times we visited, someone would invite us for Sunday lunch afterwards.

Those were quite small gestures in the grand scheme of things. Having a couple of extra people at your table, offering your spare room to visitors, being welcoming—these might not seem like much. Yet those, and the fact that the first week we were there, the pastor preached on my favorite chapter of the Bible, really helped us feel at home. We have been in that church for over a decade now.

How far does your church go to make people who speak other languages feel welcome? Do you make sure that songs are available in their languages? Are announcements printed in different languages or made available in your local sign language? Do you have Bibles available in different languages or clear instructions for people to find them on their smartphones? Do you have a welcome team or greeters who can speak more than one language or who know how to use machine interpreting devices for basic conversations? How many languages can your greeters greet people in?

Languages Are Who We Are

All of the above are about making people feel welcome. Making people feel needed goes even further. Pastor Mario Wahnschaffe points out a sad fact about migrants in churches and its solution.

> We have found that "internationals" always have one big problem in our church: I call it "spiritual unemployment."
>
> Our brothers and sisters from other countries feel paralysed by various lies:
>
> - You can't speak German correctly or well enough to serve within our congregation
> - Germany doesn't need my talents
> - Germans neither understand nor appreciate my way of thinking
> - A foreigner can't be a leader of Germans.
>
> We regularly have very talented men and women of God attending our international church services. They have been used mightily by God in their home countries, and they live up to their calling and bring their talents at our church.[2]

The greatest sign that a church feels that people who speak other languages are needed is that they are empowered to reach the full potential God has for them. Church leaders who have escaped persecution in their home countries are freed to lead in their new country. Teachers get to use their gift of teaching. Musicians get to sing and play. Doctors are freed to meet people's physical health needs. Administrators are enabled to organize. The list goes on. When people are enabled to be who God has called them to be despite speaking a different language, they feel they are needed and that they belong.

Making people feel needed and wanted therefore goes much further than making them feel welcome. It is a much, much more powerful act than simply ensuring that they can hear or see the service in their heart language. Making people feel needed and wanted means creating space for their gifts, talents, and callings, no matter which language they speak. This goes much deeper than most discussions of multilingual church, and chapters 11, 12, 14, and 15 will consider its practical application. For now, however, it is enough to remember that in our discussions of multilingual church, stopping at the provisions we make on a Sunday morning will always mean that we miss the full potential of what God has for us.

There is a third stage in the quote I cited at the beginning of this section. It pulls together everything we have examined so far. After moving

---

2 Wahnschaffe, *Building and International Church*, 429–46.

away from the idea that the church is there to help the poor migrants and telling them they are needed, Pastor Mario explained the reasoning behind all this. He said that "only they can fulfill the international vision." Put simply, the church cannot get where God wants it to go without the hearts, hands, and heads of these speakers and users of other languages that God has provided as a gift. Harvey Kwiyani puts it like this:

> Most Westerners are yet to realize this, but the heathen who need to be evangelized are in Europe today just as much as anywhere else in the world.[3]

You can just as easily substitute in your continent for Europe. North America is a mission field. South America needs Jesus. Asia and Australasia need to hear the gospel. God has chosen to use migrant Christians and migrants who will be converted to Christ through the faithful witness of multilingual churches as his instrument to bring that gospel. It remains for churches to catch this vision and pass it on to those they lead.

To ensure we don't end up replacing one human system—the homogenous unit principle—for another, the starting point has to be God. We can plant and water but only God can give the growth (1 Cor 3:6). Whatever we do as humans, whichever systems we put into place, God is the one who brings success or growth. We can do nothing of real, eternal worth without God as the first mover. A church built on the greatest research without the power of God and the fear of God will end up, at best, an empty shell. I am pleased to say that CLW was and continues to be, a growing, flourishing truly multilingual, multiracial, multicultural church. In fact, they have planted two new churches and continue to work alongside other churches with similar visions.

The Progression of Truly Multilingual Church

The quote from Pastor Mario lays out a clear progression towards becoming a church where being multilingual is a matter of identity, not just ministry. First a church decenters from focusing on those in the linguistic majority bestowing their beneficence on poor migrants. This requires having the humility to realize that we are called to build God's kingdom, not make our individual churches look good. We must accept that there is a cost in terms of our own time, money, and power. We must admit up front that there will be discomfort but accept that the burden of change cannot and should not simply be thrown on speakers and users of other languages, as if it is their job to become like us.

---

3 Kwiyani, *Multicultural Kingdom*, 10.

Decentering also means questioning the idea of a church having a dominant language and throwing out any idea that the purpose of language provision is primarily to make people more comfortable with the dominant language. Offering language lessons is fine as long as teaching migrants to fit into the local culture does not become the church's dominant goal. Remember, we are not here to teach people to fit into the world around them but to help them become more like Christ (Rom 12:1–2).

Second, a church must move from accommodating speakers and users of other languages to viewing them as people whose perspectives, talents, and voices are needed. This reinforces the idea that multilingual church is not about something we do as a program or ministry, but something we become. It means learning to share power and decision making. It means dedicating time, space, and thought to how best we can integrate the gifts of those who use different languages in our church.

Finally, a church needs to have a vision that clearly explains the purpose of decentering, in terms of reaching our local communities and the world around us. It used to be that a church would support missions by paying to send missionaries. This is still a very good idea. Increasingly, however, our mission fields might include the Polish community around the corner, the people staying in the local care home, those at the migrant processing center in a local hotel, the Chinese community nearby, or the people from the US on a study visit.

We might also add to this the fact that, while Christian missionaries may be banned from certain countries, refugees from those countries can and do meet Christ through the faithful witness of multilingual churches. When these migrants return to their homelands, they take Christ with them.

How does the vision of your church include being multilingual? Is being multilingual a necessary part of the identity, mission, vision, and values of your church? Or is it just an add-on due to a local need.

Having the humility to move away from the attitude of "helping the poor migrants" towards viewing their skills, talents, and presence as essential for the church opens the door for God to move in unexpected ways despite the necessary discomfort. Developing a vision to not just meet people's needs but release them to be who God has called them to be positions a church to truly reach, teach, and disciple the world around it.

Becoming multilingual always changes a church. If we do it in a God-honoring way, it can change us and our communities too.

The Rarity and Power of Truly Multilingual Church

I really wanted to present another clear case to end this chapter. In my head, all I had to do was to look at the research literature and cite case after case of churches getting this right and making the most of the gifted people from different cultures that God has given them. But that isn't what happened.

I found a case of a church doing a great job making interpreting a part of their identity, only to discover that the church in question was planning to ditch interpreting one day and become monolingual once and for all.[4] I found a case of an interpreter becoming personally involved in their interpreting but where one of the main purposes was to encourage people to learn the local language.[5] I found a case of interpreting being part of the identity of a church but such interpreting was only really used for visiting preachers and Bible readings.[6] I found records of churches that offer interpreting and home groups in other languages, only to find that those meetings were being used as a temporary way to look after people until they could settle into an English-speaking group.[7]

Like Korie Little Edwards in her assessment of multiethnic churches,[8] I had to conclude that, for the most part, language provision is most often seen as a means to an end, or as a tool for helping people to fit in. It seems to rarely become the powerful tool that it could be in helping people become who God made them to be, no matter the country in which they find themselves right now.

But because of CLW and because of the stories I hear from colleagues, I know that it is possible for churches to become truly, biblically multilingual. It is possible for a church to not just provide language services for the sake of integrating people into the church. They can provide such services with the purpose of enabling people to rise up to lead with the skills God has given them. In the rest of this book, we will explore ways to make that a reality in your church.

---

4 Balci Tison, "Interpreter's Involvement," 111.
5 Hokkanen, "To Serve," 40.
6 Karlik, "Interpreter-Mediated Scriptures," 164.
7 DeYmaz and Li, *Leading a Healthy*, 155.
8 Edwards, "Multiethnic Church Movement."

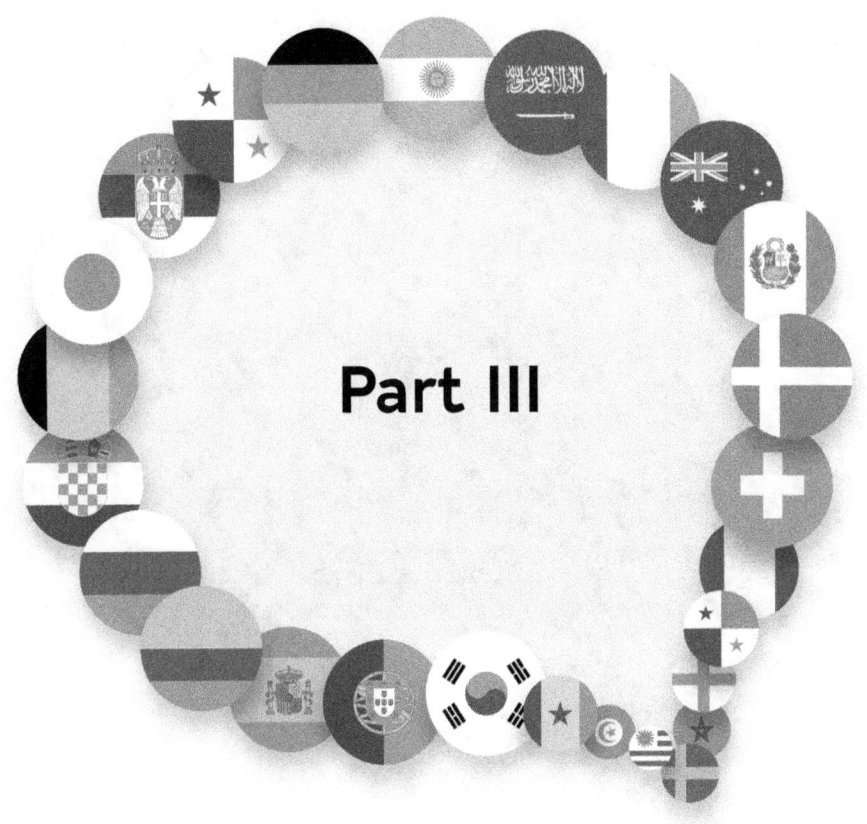

Part III

Vision, Strategy, and Implementation

CHAPTER 10

A Vision for Languages

I have read enough books myself to know that some people will have skipped the first nine chapters to get here. If that's you, welcome to the book. If you have read through those first nine chapters, this is where we turn those insights into practice. From this point on, case studies from research will take a back seat, as we turn our attention to application.

This chapter and the three following cover the practical aspects of multilingual church. While the next three chapters cover the strategy and tools available to churches and how to keep going, this chapter will cover a vital, but often missed, aspect of multilingual church—having a vision.

The Bible, the Church, and Your Church

It is worth reminding ourselves of the wider vision that God has for the Church. The whole Bible testifies to the centrality of Christ and to the fact that God's plan is that "at the right time he will bring everything together under the authority of Christ—everything in heaven and on earth." (Eph 1:10, NLT). This bringing of everything together is represented by the worship of Christ in heaven by people from every nation and tribe and people and language (Rev 7:9). This is the lamb who was slain before the foundation of the world (Rev 13:8). This is also the lion of the tribe of Judah (Rev 5:5), who alone is worthy to open the scrolls of God's plan and of the unfolding of history.

> God's plan is to build a worldwide Church, where there are no barriers between us and God and between us and each other.

Because Christ is the worthy lamb who was slain, who receives worship from every nation and tribe and people and language, God has sent his people out with the ministry of reconciliation (2 Cor 5:10–21), calling people to be reconciled to God. Notice that Paul frames his work and our work as Christ's ambassadors within the wider plan of God's justice. If the love of Christ compelled Paul, in light of God's goodness and judgment, to proclaim God's reconciliation to the world, why would that message have any lesser effect on us?

God's plan is to build a worldwide Church, where there are no barriers between us and God and between us and each other. As we discussed in chapter 2, it is entirely against the thrust of the story and teachings of the early church to read this as all nations and tribes and peoples and languages praising Christ in their own, segregated communities.

No, as the book of Galatians makes abundantly clear, God's plan is that the church would be a house where all nations pray and praise and worship together. We cannot demonstrate the wisdom of God to a world fractured by segregation, division, and separation if our churches show exactly the same segregation, division, and separation. Instead, the Church is to be the place where "the wisdom of God in its rich variety might now be made known to the rulers and authorities in the heavenly places" (Eph 3:10, NRSV). This is specifically the wisdom of God's plan in which "the Gentiles have become fellow-heirs, members of the same body, and sharers in the promise in Christ Jesus through the gospel" (Eph 3:6, NRSV).

> **We cannot demonstrate the wisdom of God to a world fractured by segregation, division, and separation if our churches show exactly the same segregation, division, and separation.**

We can explain Paul's logic like this: the Church and individual churches demonstrate to the physical and spiritual world the wisdom and love of God by being places where there is such radical unity between people of wildly different social, cultural, and linguistic backgrounds that people cannot help but stand back and gasp in awe. This powerful demonstration of the wisdom and love of God is an example of God's kingdom on earth. It gives us a foretaste of heaven itself and shows our obedience to Jesus's commands to love God and our neighbor (Matt 22:34–39; Luke 10:25–37). In fact, this is part of making disciples of all nations (Matt 28:18–20)—a commission that is based on Jesus having all authority in heaven and on earth.

This is just a tiny overview of the vast wisdom and overwhelming glory of God's plan and purpose for the church. Any vision that we might have for individual churches has to align with this plan. This is God's vision with which we are called to align our work.

With God's vision for the church in mind, what does it mean to have a vision for language in the church you lead? As we saw in chapter 8, a vision on its own is rarely enough, no matter how emotive and powerful the vision might be. If God's vision for the church reminds us of the church's mission, something similar might apply to our churches today.

For Paul, certainly, God's vision for the church compelled him to keep on proclaiming the gospel and planting and supporting churches. His life

A Vision for Languages

was about joining in with what God was already doing, with his eyes fixed on Jesus and on the promises of God for the future. The same applies to your church. The vision your church has for languages, inasmuch as it aligns with God's vision, gives meaning to the work as you partner with God in the work he is already doing.

Why Vision for Languages Matters

Churches without a vision for languages tend to think in terms of the cheapest or easiest solution or the one-off shortcut. A lack of vision or a vision that does not have a specific and explicit place for languages across the life of the church leads to churches getting stuck in less-than-ideal approaches, like those discussed in chapters 3–8. Yet a vision with no change in action, thinking, or belief also misses the mark. This chapter only discusses vision, but it should be read alongside the next two chapters on strategy and mechanics. Vision is about setting our direction. Strategy and mechanics are about how we get moving.

So, let's set the direction. Instead of dictating what your vision should look like, the next section will offer some questions to ask and explain why their answers matter.

Starting Questions: Where Are You Now?

The first set of questions helps to set the vision by clarifying where you are right now. Even if you're going in the right direction, you will get lost without a good idea of your current location. I once got lost trying to follow directions to a meeting in a church. I had taken the wrong exit from the train station and so started on completely the wrong side of the tracks. I followed the directions but with the wrong starting point.

Similarly, I can offer all the training on interpreting technology, using different languages in church, and preaching with an interpreter that I like but, if the church is already half-way through a contract with a major remote interpreting provider or has already decided to offer different services in different languages, then that training will be pointless. So how do you gauge where you are now? Try asking your leadership team questions like these and ask a selection of church members for their thoughts.

1. Which languages are already used in your church?
2. Which languages are used in your surrounding community?
3. What outreach work do you already have among people who speak different languages and how well-established is that?

4. Are there people who are either in the church or who would like to come to church who use a different language at home than your locally dominant language?
5. What are you currently doing to reach, teach, and disciple people who speak different languages?
6. How open is the congregation to having people who speak different languages in the church?
7. How readily does your congregation welcome challenge, change, or internal disagreement?
8. How united is the entire leadership team, from the senior leadership to home group, children's, youth, and other group leaders about the value of making your church more welcoming to people who speak different languages?

As you can see, few of these are simple "yes or no" questions. Many of them could easily be broken down into several parts. In fact, it is likely that answering some of those questions will require some honest conversations. If nothing else, considering becoming a multilingual church might be a way to help churches foster a culture of honesty and listening to other perspectives without judgment. Once those questions have been answered, it's time to think about the resources available. Even Jesus instructed us to count the cost before undertaking a project (Luke 14:28–30). It is wonderful to believe God for a miracle of provision of equipment or finances, but often God wants us to be faithful with the little we already have (Luke 16:10). Here are some key resource questions:

1. How many people currently attend your church on a typical Sunday?
2. How many of the people in your church speak or sign another language to the point where they can have a conversation with a native speaker?
3. How many people in your church have qualifications in any modern spoken or signed language, including ones in translation and interpreting?
4. Looking at your church finances, if income and expenses behave in line with how they have in previous years, is the church expected to have a surplus, break even or lose money? If it is expected to have a surplus or lose money, how much of a surplus or a loss is forecasted?

5. What equipment do you have for sound and video? How many people in the church are trained to use this equipment?
6. Is your church already live streaming services? If so, how much do you know about the people who join you online?
7. How many people in your church, and especially on the leadership team, have experience in missions, cross-cultural evangelism and discipleship, or building multicultural teams in the workplace?
8. How does your congregation react to change?
9. How diverse is your congregation in terms of age, income, race, sex, educational background, and culture?
10. How does your congregation react when someone comes into the church who is from a different background than the one they are used to?
11. If your church is already offering language provision, how committed, trained, and energetic are the people involved?
12. Is pastoral care set up for people involved in language provision?

Notice the overlap between questions about where a church is now and the resources it has available. We might be tempted to "despise these small beginnings" (Zech 4:10, NLT), but God always starts with what we already have and where we already are. Honesty is essential here. It is much easier to cast a big vision about feeding the crowds than to face the fact that you only have five loaves and two fish—and Jesus. It is more inspiring to talk about where you will be in ten years than to face the facts of where you are now.

But, if we are going to receive a God-honoring vision, we must first face up to where we are now. Once we have looked at where we are as a church, alongside who and what we have as a church, we can start to think clearly, not about where we want to be in five years or ten years, but about where we go next.

None of this planning or consideration should in any way be taken as a lack of faith or as an excuse for not seeing past slow, incremental growth. Jesus absolutely takes our faith like a mustard seed and causes extraordinary growth. But it honors God and honors people if we take account of where we are, who we have, and what we have. Once we know where we are now, we can begin to think about our destination and what getting there might look like.

Doing so requires looking at identity and priority questions. Many leaders are more comfortable here. This is where you get to explore the vision God gave you for the church and what it means. Let's start with the God-given identity of the church.

Development Questions: Identity and Priorities

1. What are the key verses of Scripture that your church is based on?
2. What is the mission or vision statement of your church?
3. How does that statement play out in an ordinary week?
4. What visions or prophecies are relevant to your church?
5. If you had to pick three words that sum up the values of your church, what would they be? If members of your congregation were to do the same, what would they say?
6. Which Scriptures or topics tend to be preached the most regularly in your church?
7. What is the first thing someone notices when they come into one of your church services?
8. What is the unique calling that God has for your church?
9. If your church no longer existed, what would the community around it miss?
10. Aside from generic words like "church" and "Christian" and anything to do with location, what do you think would be the most appropriate online search terms someone could use to find your church?

The language provision that will suit a given church is as dependent on who the church is and who God has called them to be as on budget or vision. For example, a church that God has called to carry the torch of tradition, ceremony, and ancient modes of worship into a new generation might find that using translated liturgies, adopting some formalisms from other countries, or hiring leaders who speak different languages might suit them well.

Conversely, a church that is called to "sing a new song of praise" to the Lord (Ps 33:3) by innovative forms of presentation, teaching, and even service structure will tend to find it more useful to look for agile forms of language provision, such as live subtitling, or interpreting provided by humans, either professionals or people within the congregation.

A Vision for Languages

The end goal is the same and the vision might even be similar, but the unique identity that God has given to the church will determine the tools that are best for them. Once again, the purpose is not to somehow systematize God out of the equation. Neither is it about trying to lead purely by human reason. Instead, it is about honoring the uniqueness of each church and wisely choosing from among the many tools that God has given us. We are all part of the same body, but we are not all the same.

Our different identities mean that we have different priorities. The following priority questions aim to help you think about where your church should be going next on the journey towards becoming multilingual.

1. If the people in your congregation were told they could either be comfortable without any further spiritual or numerical growth, or they could grow spiritually and numerically but would have to be happy with being uncomfortable, which would they choose?
2. Looking at an average week in your church, does more effort go into discipling people who are already in the church or into reaching people not currently attending?
3. What needs do you see in your community that your church is passionate about meeting?
4. How important would you say multilingualism is for your church? Is it part of your ongoing vision and mission, a ministry you would like to start, a need that you are looking to fulfill, a drag on resources, or something else?
5. Does the entire leadership team share the same or a similar vision for the church becoming multilingual?
6. How much change would your church be prepared to walk through for the sake of becoming multilingual?
7. How much discomfort would the people in your congregation be happy to experience for the same cause?
8. If you were to list the top ten priorities for the church, where would "becoming multilingual" be on that list?
9. If someone in your church was not being discipled due to language differences, how would the church react?

It is vital at this point to stress that there are no wrong answers. It is also important to stress that clear, but uncomfortable answers are better than answers that dance around the question. It is quite likely that some leaders will answer these questions and realize that the church lacks the resources, people, identity, commitment, or vision to become multilingual. That is fine. The reality is that not all churches can or should become multilingual. Yet, there are some churches to whom God has given a biblical conviction to be able to reach, teach, and disciple the people in their community, no matter which language they speak. For those churches, these questions are intended to provoke thought about how best to do so and where to start.

Before actually doing any work, the leadership may need to spend some time teaching on the biblical call to reconciliation, living as one body with different parts, and loving those who are different from us. Some churches are ready to dive into anything, and simply need to spend time in prayer and worship, seeking God for what to do next. I also know of churches that are already offering some language provision but need to think carefully about their next steps. The questions in this chapter, if thought through carefully and answered honestly, could be a helpful guide through that journey.

Any church that is looking to offer language provision will soon find that it has to be a part of the wider vision, identity, and values of the church. As discussed in chapter 7, when language provision is just something that happens because it has to or because someone feels like offering it, it tends to wither quickly. Yet, when it becomes part of the church's identity, it becomes a powerful tool.

One last question needs to be answered before we consider creating and then implementing a strategy for language provision.

The Vision Question

Given the answers to the questions in this chapter, what vision has God given you regarding language provision to allow you to reach, teach, and disciple the people in your community?

This seems a fairly broad question. It might help to think about it in this way: what will your church look like with language provision? What impact will language provision have on your church and its surrounding community?

Of course, having a vision is wonderful but, at some point, vision has to lead to action. In the next two chapters, we will discuss strategy—the "when and where" of language provision—and options for implementation—the "how and who."

CHAPTER 11

Strategy—The When and Where

Strategy before mechanics: that's always the right order. I have written, spoken, and taught some variation of that phrase quite a lot over the past year. Somewhere between the kinds of kingdom vision that many churches love (chapter 10) and the questions of exactly how to physically provide language access in church meetings (chapter 12) comes this awkward, rarely mentioned, stage called strategy.

If you come from the same charismatic tradition as I do, strategy may seem like a dirty word. Aren't we supposed to be standing in faith and leaving the details to God? Does having a human strategy mean that we are putting our faith in humans? It's not much better in some other traditions. Some Christians might argue that things are successful because God willed them to work so strategy is about us trying to wrestle control from God. Others might see strategy as an unwelcome visitor from the corporate world that always brings with it the ugly specter of Key Performance Indicators, Gantt charts, and (shiver!) spreadsheets.

> *Strategy before mechanics: that's always the right order.*

Yet strategy need not create fear. Neither does strategy have to be some weak attempt to out-plan God. If we see strategy simply as the step between the vision and the everyday choices, its value becomes clear.

Planning the Journey

A few days before writing this chapter, my wife and I came home to Edinburgh from a holiday in a town on the west coast of Scotland called Wemyss Bay. Since the public transport on that route is fairly reliable and since we currently don't have a car, we plotted a route home that involved two trains and a bus. There were several options.

Without children, the most comfortable and fastest option is to catch the train from Wemyss Bay to Glasgow Central, walk the 10 minutes or so to Glasgow Queen Street and then take the express train to Edinburgh Waverly. From that station, there is then a direct bus to our house. In fact, we did that exact route in reverse on the way to our holiday, with a little lunchtime pit stop in Glasgow on the way.

But on the way home from the holiday, we were tired, our children were tired, one child's suitcase was broken and emotions were not exactly at their best. So we changed our strategy. After taking the train to Glasgow Central from Wemyss Bay, we got a direct, although much slower, train from Glasgow Central to Edinburgh. It added a good 25 minutes to our journey time but it meant much less walking and a lot less stress.

A strategy is simply a journey plan.

A strategy is simply a journey plan. We knew where we wanted to go (vision) and had decided to use mostly trains (implementation), but exactly which trains and their routing was still a choice we had to make. That choice of how to use the tools available to get to the destination we have in mind is strategy.

Strategy and Multilingual Church—Thinking through "When"

What does strategy look like for multilingual churches? Strategy is the journey plan for when and where the church will offer language provision. The actual tools available and who can provide them is the subject of the next chapter. Yet it is worth the time to dwell on the fact that the "when" and "where" are important questions in their own right. Let's start with "when."

Questions around "when" require us to think through the scenarios when offering language provision will be important to the work the church is doing and, more importantly, to the welcoming and discipleship of those in the church. The question of when language provision is offered is a very practical one: What language provision will be offered at which church meetings or events?

This kind of question can quickly become complicated. Whenever I am asked about language provision outside of Sunday services, I find myself wanting to answer that question with some questions of my own. Anyone can say something simple like "machine interpreting is useful in home groups," but the truth is that it might not be. It might be that the best thing to do is to have home groups in different languages and only offer interpreting on Sunday services. It might be that the opposite is sometimes more useful, with interpreting only offered in home groups, while Sundays are monolingual.

The answers will depend on the vision and values of the church, the people who currently attend and their needs, the church's budget, and the skills and competencies available within the church. There are no perfect answers but there are quite a few wrong ones. Or rather, there are quite a few wrong ways to try to answer the question.

How Do We View Those Who Speak Different Languages?

For a church to have a helpful, biblical language strategy, we need to have a helpful, biblical view of people who speak different languages. As I mentioned in chapter 9, in the research for this book, I came across the view that home groups in migrant languages were a temporary stepping stone towards deeper integration into the wider church.[1] The question there was how to balance people's need to be around those who spoke their language with the eventual necessity (according to some) for people to speak their language less in church, as they adapt to the wider church.

> For a church to have a helpful, biblical language strategy, we need to have a helpful, biblical view of people who speak different languages.

This view, whether intentionally or not, operates from the clear assumption that languages are barriers. Churches can fret about the possibility of migrant language home groups turning into language-based cliques far more than they worry about the church itself becoming a clique or any other part of the church becoming its own little group. It is as if people still using *their* languages on a regular basis within the church is a sign of them not being fully committed to the church.

Indeed, sometimes the questions we ask about multilingual church reflect this assumption. Often, we can spend time thinking through how we can help people learn the dominant languages of our countries and yet not think as much about what we miss when we don't allow people to exercise their God-given gifts until they learn our language. Offering language classes can be helpful to migrants unless those classes become a condition for membership or for serving in the church.

When we impose language-based limits, we stop walking in the reality of Pentecost or the freedom proclaimed by the Jerusalem Council. We want to avoid having churches that reflect the same power imbalances and injustices as the world around us, when we should biblically oppose them. If we are not careful, we can end up building ways to help people become more like the world, forgetting that part of our message is not to be conformed to the world (Rom 12:1–2).

There is one further point worth considering. Those who use the dominant language can demonstrate our love and welcome by learning the languages of those in the church. What better way to welcome and include people than by learning the language they already use?

---

1 DeYmaz and Li, *Leading a Healthy*, 155.

For churches, integrating people together should be about everyone becoming more like Christ (Eph 4:1–16), not making *them* become like *us*. Chapter 9 explained that this includes being open to people from other countries having leadership gifts the church needs, even if, or perhaps especially when those gifts mean the church changing in some way. The greatest sign that a church values users of other languages is helping them grow in the church to reach their full potential. This core message of chapter 9 is the foundation of any good strategy for a church to become multilingual, especially when we consider when language provision will be available.

Worrying that language provision will foster division and trying to use language provision as a temporary service are poor foundations for language strategy. Both are based on the view that the dominant language is better, more holy, or even just the main marker of what it means to be part of a certain church. This mindset turns language ability into an excuse for the kind of favoritism that the book of James warns us against (Jas 2:1–13), especially as, in most countries, people who are not fluent in the dominant language tend to be poorer.

Answering the question of *when* we provide language services therefore means asking whether we want to offer language provision as something we do for migrants who need our help, or as something we do for the good of everyone in the church, so we can all grow together. Don't misunderstand: there are many circumstances where speakers of different languages do have material, physical, or emotional needs due to what they have suffered before they arrive. Caring for the needs of migrants, especially refugees, is entirely biblical and can be an important part of the strategies we create to become multilingual. In fact, asking which languages are used in poverty relief work is vital.

Yet equating the use of a different language to someone being needy or lacking is highly problematic. Similarly problematic is the view that language provision is something we do to make others more comfortable with our way of operating. Both sound caring but can easily become paternalistic and ultimately, self-defeating.

Everyone can tell the difference between being valued and being put down. Being valued makes people feel welcome, even though they might be conscious of their differences. When we show that we value people by offering them help and discipleship tailored to their needs, then they are likely to stay. When people feel that our assistance is coming from a place of seeing them as less valuable or less important, then they will naturally want to walk away.

Another, often unnoticed, issue is that people can relate differently to different languages, even when they use all of them fluently. I have been using French in some shape or form since around the age of 8 and have been able to hold a conversation in it since my late teens. I can listen to sermons and podcasts and watch films in French comfortably, as you might expect from an interpreter. However, if you want me to catch information quickly or to be emotionally affected by something, English is still the much better option. I could attend a French church with no issues and would understand everything that was said and sung. Yet nothing would hit me in quite the same way as it would in the language I lived with growing up.

Answering the "When" Question: A Summary

Answering the question of when language provision is offered is not about what is most comfortable for the church. It is about listening to and responding to the language needs of those in the church and aligning this provision with the resources, commitment, and readiness of the membership. Our strategies for language provision must consider the needs, desires, values, and willingness of those who are already in the church, especially if they speak the locally dominant language. Language provision strategies also need to take into account the needs, desires, and skills of users of other languages, as well as the vision of the church. The importance of users of the locally dominant language will be discussed in more detail later (chapter 14). For now, I will simply note that strategies for language provision involve everyone and must explicitly include when the locally dominant language will be used.

All these considerations circle back to one simple question: when will the different language provision tools be used in your church?

You could decide that every meeting will still be in the locally dominant language. If there are speakers of different languages in the congregation, I cannot honesty recommend this, for reasons that should be obvious by now. I do honor churches who make this decision purposefully and for solid reasons. I would ask them to consider whether they are doing so for the right biblical reasons or for the sake of comfort and ease.

Your church could decide to just use a single strategy for every meeting. This might mean that every meeting is only available in one language, but that this language changes. There might be three Sunday services in three different languages and three different sets of home groups or prayer groups or Bible study groups, each in different languages. Perhaps every single meeting is interpreted.

Most likely, churches will choose to mix and match what is available when. Some churches might even change their language provision across the church calendar. Certainly, it is not unknown for special services to be interpreted by professionals, while others are interpreted in-house or left monolingual. Home groups, Bible study groups, and prayer groups can be monolingual, interpreted by humans or by machines, or multilingual in some other way. Websites can be monolingual, fully translated, partially translated, translated by humans, volunteers or even by machine—although the fact that Google routinely down rates machine translated websites[2] and that such websites almost always contain errors mean that I cannot recommend that last option.

The actual strategy for when different kinds of language provision are offered is almost always less important than the work that goes into getting that strategy right. There are no perfect solutions. Every choice has its advantages and disadvantages, but it is vital to choose deliberately and, dare I say it, strategically, and to follow through and be flexible enough to change if necessary. Better to do something deliberately and well than to wait to find the perfect solution and end up doing nothing.

This discussion simply covers the "when"—the meetings, events, conversations, and times at which some kind of deliberate language provision is available. What about "where"? Why might location matter?

Thinking through "Where"

Questions around "where" are, in some ways, far simpler than questions around "when." Answering "when" often involves thinking through every single meeting or interaction that someone might have with a church and asking what language provision works best.

Answering "where" comes down to one question: How does the location of a church meeting or event affect the language provision offered?

The answer to this question might include offering an interpreter for street evangelism. It might mean providing translated Bible study materials or translating the church website. It might mean offering multilingual subtitling for church live streams. It could mean figuring out what language provision is needed in home groups.

Thinking through "where" includes considering where those delivering the language provision will be while they work. This consideration covers the distinction between remote and in-person interpreting which appears

---

2 Google Search Central, "Spam Policies."

in the next chapter, as well as questions around the use of translators inside the church versus agencies.

The precise choices made by each church will be different. For churches using language provision to reach new people, it makes sense for most of this provision to start outside of the church building, with a translated website, interpreted street evangelism, and some kind of language provision during other outreach activities. For churches addressing the needs of those already in the church, targeting home groups, Sunday services, and perhaps pastoral counselling might make more sense.

Strategy in Action

There are no one-size-fits-all solutions. The meaning of "multilingual church" will necessarily change from one church to another. What matters more is being intentional and thinking through the options and the direction of the church, rather than just throwing something together.

Two examples from earlier in the book help to explain why strategy matters so much more than mechanics. Remember the church from chapter 8 who hadn't arranged for any French discipleship resources? They did the right thing in getting expert help to ensure that the interpreting was delivered excellently, but they stopped there. Just delivering interpreting, without connecting it to the rest of the event or even to the rest of their strategy for ensuring that new converts were given the right discipleship resources left a significant gap. This is an incredibly easy mistake to make and one that happens any time a church thinks about how to offer language provision without asking tough questions about their language strategy and wider vision for languages. Strategy before mechanics.

And what about the PEAS project from chapter 7? The reason why it worked so well with the police and not the NHS was precisely that the police didn't just have a strategy for the project, but for sign language more broadly. In fact, they used the project to develop and improve that strategy. The NHS meanwhile, got the mechanics of setting up the project and getting the right permissions in place but never connected the dots to make a coherent project strategy. Good strategic thinking honors God and honors the people he has put in our care.

CHAPTER 12

Implementation—The How and Who

I am reasonably sure that, for many readers, this chapter will be the reason they bought the book. As a consultant interpreter, the vast majority of the questions I am asked revolve around how to implement interpreting. When I have done webinars on church interpreting, most of the questions have focused on whether one solution or another will work in a given situation. That is natural. I hope, however, that the eleven chapters before this one have been enough to convince readers that picking between simultaneous and consecutive interpreting, or even between having different services in different languages and using artificial intelligence, is not the biggest decision churches face.

Vision comes before strategy. Strategy comes before mechanics. This chapter will discuss the mechanics of multilingual church. But I have to stress again that the best mechanics in the world are not enough. Mechanics only work when they are part of a bigger vision, strategy, and theological commitment. With that in mind, let's go over the main options.

Option 1: Do Nothing

Doing nothing is the simplest option. In monolingual communities, this is, understandably, the default option. In other communities, churches can see the multilingualism around them and choose to keep their services in the locally dominant language. We have already looked at what this feels like in chapter 3. It is worth mentioning that with this approach, churches might find themselves dealing with language difference anyway.

Churches who choose this option might want to think about offering language classes or adjusting the complexity of language used in their services, to accommodate those whose knowledge of the locally dominant language is weaker.

It is also important to note that doing nothing is itself a choice. In multilingual communities, it is a choice that excludes people, even if that is not the aim. This choice may be justified for small churches that lack the volunteer or financial resources to commit to multilingualism. In such circumstances, partnering with congregations who use different languages in their services can be an important community outreach tool. That brings us to the second option.

Option 2: Hold Different Services in Different Languages

This option was discussed at length in chapter 4. While there are issues with holding different services in different languages, churches looking to do so have access to some useful resources. There are books covering models of multiethnic church that provide useful information on this kind of multilingualism.[1]

There are a few conditions that need to be met to make this option viable for a church. There must be enough people who want to attend such services. This might mean having those people in the church already or having trained leaders and evangelists in those languages who can bring people in. It could also mean partnering with an existing church that uses that language. One way or another, people need to come to services in different languages for them to work.

The next requirement is space, both in terms of physical space and in terms of a time slot. Some churches might feel that they can best manage space by having the different services take place at different times. The challenge in that case is ensuring that the people still feel like they belong to the same church and not different churches meeting in the same building.

Other churches might prefer to have all of their language services take place at the same time. In such cases, the challenge is to find the right physical spaces for all the services. Offering services in one language in a huge, airy space while the people attending another service squash into a cramped room is hardly a demonstration of our unity in Christ. Subdividing one room also leads to issues of sound leakage and disturbance.

The biggest question around different services in different languages is not attendance or space, but leadership. As discussed in chapter 4, such services can easily end up creating new churches, rather than different meetings of the same church. Therefore, it is vital that any attempt to host different services in different languages is accompanied by equal efforts to create a multilingual leadership team with equality among the members. Somehow, a common church identity and vision needs to flow across all services. Time also needs to be spent in finding ways to help those who attend the different services to meet each other and build relationships across languages.

In this case, the "how" of finding space and time to create different services in different languages and the "why" of creating a unified church identity and vision relates closely to many "who" questions. Who will lead

---

1 DeYmaz and Li, *Leading a Healthy*; Garces-Foley, *Crossing the Ethnic Divide*.

these services? Who will be on the leadership team of the entire church? Answering these questions sets the foundations for having different services in different languages.

Option 3: Integrate Different Languages into the Same Service

Chapter 5 examined the experience of having different services in different languages. It is worth thinking through the "how" and "who" of this option more closely. What might this actually look like in a church?

Carefully integrating different languages into the same service is no easy task. This is one case where questions around how to deliver such language provision will dominate the conversation.

Like it or not, different parts of a church service have different symbolic meanings and different levels of importance for those in the service. Leaving the announcements in a locally dominant language tells people that only those speaking that language are supposed to hear about what is going on. Only ever preaching in the locally dominant language can easily become both a theological statement about which languages God speaks in and a practical statement about who the primary audience of the sermon is.

Liturgical churches have the advantage here. In some such churches, there are translations of entire liturgies into other languages. All that is needed then is for someone to download the relevant liturgy in the required languages, print out what is needed and make those copies available. With the addition of some translated announcements and a translation of the sermon or homily, the language needs of the congregation can be covered every Sunday.

Translation Options

Translating the announcements and sermon or homily then becomes an important concern. There are three options available. If there are people in the church with the right skills, the translation can be done by members of the church. A useful system would be for one person to do the translation while someone else revises the translation and checks for errors before printing. Using volunteers is often a very cheap option but takes time. A professional translator can manage between two and three thousand words per day. This is roughly equal to 16.5 to 25 minutes of speech. Someone without professional training is unlikely to produce nearly that much.

Using in-house translation therefore requires both the sermon and announcements to be with the translators at least two or three days before they are printed. Translators may also have questions about the translation, especially for preachers who like to use jokes or local stories, which can take additional time to resolve.

It is possible to reduce this time using Computer Aided Translation (CAT) tools, which remember how sentences have been translated in the past and suggest these previous versions to the translator. Such software is especially useful when a church has a regular calendar of events or when the meetings each week are largely the same. In such cases, once the schedule has been translated, subsequent announcements can be translated with only minimal changes, saving time.

The time savings of CAT tools are not as significant for sermons but, where preachers like to use similar phrases or where common call and response or liturgical elements are used, CAT software will speed up translation.

Translating text in-house, even with CAT tools, should not be confused with the second option, which is Machine Translation (MT). MT uses computers to translate the entire document with little to no human help and produces translations much more quickly than any human ever could. An entire sermon could be translated almost as soon as it is copy and pasted into the system.

But MT has flaws. Public MT systems, such as Google Translate or Microsoft Translator, are not specifically set up for churches. With Christian content, it tends to skew towards the most common denomination represented in the dataset of the language it is translating into. It might even use vocabulary from other religions. In a quick experiment, I found that Google Translate into French tends to produce Roman Catholic terminology, rather than Protestant terminology.

For this reason, it is very common for MT to be checked and corrected by professionals or local experts afterwards, leading to Post-Edited Machine Translation (PEMT). PEMT tends to take less time than fully human translation and can produce acceptable results. However, apart from very predictable contexts, it will not rival the results of specialist human translators. It may, however, produce results that are comparable to the work of untrained translators.

PEMT will therefore be most useful when the church has speakers of the language who are not quite able to produce high-quality translations. It is also helpful in contexts where, for whatever reason, the translation has to be produced at short notice. It will definitely miss any wordplay, struggle with jokes and local stories, and will likely produce translations that appear rather flat and matter of fact.

The third option is to use professional translators for all texts in other languages. This has the advantage that professionals will almost certainly have access to CAT tools and will know how to use them effectively. A specialized professional will also know how churches work and their turnaround requirements. Some may even be specialized in your specific denomination, although this is quite rare.

Most professionals will be able to offer a service where their work is checked by another expert before it reaches the client. This means that the document arrives ready to print. Modern professional CAT tools even allow for preserving layout and formatting so there is no need to copy and paste the translation into another document.

Of course, professionals will need to be paid. It is still common for professionals to bill per word or per thousand words in the original text. In some countries per page or per line billing is more common. A good translator or translation agency should be able to advise on how to reduce the final bill through, for example, creating a standard format for announcements or inserting the translations of any Scriptures verses before the file goes to the translator.

Translation by a specialized professional will always produce the best results, but it is the most expensive option and will be out of reach for many churches. Knowing that, raising up in-house volunteers or staff to do the task would seem like a very useful option. The final chapter of this book lists good places to look for training.

Solutions beyond Translation

Translation is a very useful option for liturgical churches. But for churches without a set liturgy, providing a written translation of the entire service is not an option. In these cases, as suggested in chapter 5, singing songs in other languages, inviting people to pray in other languages (perhaps with a translation projected onto a screen), and even inviting people to preach in other languages might be a helpful way forward. The main thing is to find a way to publicly honor and value other languages in a way that is meaningful for everyone.

Beyond translation, simply having different languages heard from the front of the church is important. Having someone pray in a different language, learning songs in a different language, and even hearing the odd sermon that is not in the locally dominant language are powerful signs that the church sees languages as signs of belonging rather than barriers. Let me be perfectly clear, having different languages in the same service can and should challenge the dominance of the locally dominant language. Challenging this dominance is good and biblical.

Working through how different languages can be heard and seen on stage is a complicated task for any multilingual church, no matter which other options are used. Yes, it will make some people uncomfortable, but discomfort is often a sign of growth. Yes, it takes planning and effort to get right but so do most things. However else your church becomes multilingual, integrating different languages into every part of church life will be a step in that process.

Integrating lots of languages into one service does mean that people will need to have a way to understand what is being said. The next option is by far the most detailed, since it involves many different choices. Departing from the order used earlier in the book, the next section will cover every single option that churches have regarding interpreting. Some of these are likely to be ones that churches have not considered but all of them come with their own distinct challenges and potential.

Option 4: Interpreting

What Is Interpreting Anyway?

Before we go through all the interpreting options churches have, we need to remind ourselves what interpreting is. Interpreting takes place while an event, meeting, or indeed church service or conference is ongoing. Translation comes after something has been completed: such as after a document has been written or the video has been edited or the web page has been designed. That difference explains why there are so many different options for churches to use interpreting. It also explains why using interpreting well involves practices that happen long before and long after the church meeting or conference even starts.

One useful way to divide these options into understandable chunks is to start by how the interpreting takes place. This gives us two main approaches or "modes": simultaneous interpreting and consecutive interpreting. Both of these modes can be delivered in the same place as the church service or meeting is happening, which we will call "in-person interpreting." Alternatively, they can also be delivered in a different place from the meeting or event and accessed via internet, satellite, or phone. This is called remote interpreting. That makes four options: remote simultaneous, remote consecutive, in-person consecutive, and in-person simultaneous. In-person simultaneous can also be delivered with or without specialist equipment, so that one will be left to last. Let's consider these options individually.

Remote Simultaneous Interpreting (RSI)

This form of interpreting exploded during the pandemic and not just in church. When people were mostly locked down, interpreters found they could still do their work, with a few adjustments, while sitting at home.

Remote Simultaneous Interpreting (RSI) works like this.

First, the people at the interpreted event or meeting create an online live stream. This is exactly what many churches did during the pandemic. Next, the stream is connected to some means of sending it to an interpreter or interpreters. Ways to do this vary from simply sending the interpreter a YouTube link (not ideal), to creating a video conference call and using the inbuilt interpreter module in platforms such as Zoom, Microsoft Teams, or Citrix to connect to the interpreter (better). Another option is to contract with a specialist RSI provider (usually best but often quite expensive).

Finally, the church makes the video with the interpreter's audio (or video, for sign language interpreting) available for people to listen to or watch. This can be done with some kind of audio broadcasting software, creating a second YouTube stream, inviting people to connect to a video conference, or using the inbuilt capabilities of any RSI platform. Sometimes, these solutions can even be combined, with the output of the RSI platform being added to a YouTube stream.

If this all seems complicated, it helps to think of it in three stages:

1. Get good quality audio and video set up
2. Provide a channel for sending that to the interpreters
3. Provide a channel for people to see or hear what the interpreters produce

No matter how a church chooses to follow these instructions, the result is that people can hear or see the interpreting wherever they are. RSI allows a church to have simultaneous interpreting without either the high equipment costs or high amounts of disruption caused by in-person simultaneous interpreting. This makes RSI incredibly flexible—it works just as well for those in the service using an internet enabled device as it does for people attending online. RSI also scales exceptionally well and can be used to offer any number of languages at the same time.

RSI also has the advantage of making interpreting available wherever and whenever it is needed. Finding local interpreters to work in your church could be a challenge since those who really know what they are doing will most likely be working in their own churches while your services are going on. Asking interpreters to travel from further away is expensive and probably still means that they will miss their own services. RSI uses the unappreciated blessing of time differences to unlock a much wider pool of interpreters. With RSI, the pool of available help becomes global.

Here's a simple example. When I am interpreting for a church via RSI, the church will almost always be a few thousand miles and a handful of time zones behind me. So, on a Sunday when I am interpreting, I attend the service in my own church, come home, eat lunch, do my interpreting preparation and then, just as my family is thinking about dinner, I log on to an interpreting platform and proceed to interpret for the 11am or 1pm service for a church in a completely different country. Sure, I still haven't quite gotten used to interpreting "Good morning, church" into French when I am thinking about Sunday dinner, but it means that I provide interpreting without leaving the house. The churches I work with get access to a specialist interpreter thousands of miles away.

RSI is especially useful when there are few, or even no, local interpreters for a particular language. If a church were to call me and ask to find them English to Spanish church interpreters here in Edinburgh, I would struggle. However, it just so happens that I know many who are located in the USA and Central America. RSI gives the church access to them too.

The Disadvantages of RSI

Despite its advantages, RSI has well-documented issues and strict technological requirements. In terms of the issues, interpreters lose concentration more quickly in RSI than they do in any other mode.[2] When interpreters lose concentration, the quality of their interpreting drops. This is because simultaneous interpreting involves listening, analyzing, speaking or signing, and monitoring your own work, all at the same time.[3] Therefore, it is not a good idea to ask one interpreter to work on an entire service on their own. While this is true in any mode, it is especially important in RSI. To ensure that the interpreting remains excellent throughout the service or meeting, two interpreters per language are needed. Those interpreters will also need some way to communicate with each other.

Another issue with RSI is that interpreters can often feel distant from what they are trying to interpret.[4] This might sound like a minor

---

2 Braun and Taylor, "Video-Mediated Interpreting," 33–68.
3 Gile, *Basic Concepts and Models*, 167–74.
4 Mouzourakis, "Remote Interpreting," 45–66; Napier, Skinner, and Turner, "It's Good for Them," 1–23.

issue but it does have important implications for churches. One of the lesser-known techniques used by interpreters involves adjusting how they interpret according to the situation. This might mean omitting information they know that the audience already knows so they can save mental capacity for more important sections,[5] explaining culture-specific details,[6] strategically choosing which Bible translation to use, or choosing the right way of interpreting something the speaker said among the many possible alternatives. Such decisions rely on what the interpreter knows about the speaker, the audience, and the situation.

Remove the interpreter from the situation, take away their ability to see if people are understanding what is being said or signed and you limit their ability to make those kinds of fine adjustments. My PhD supervisor, Professor Graham Turner, would often call interpreting "the negotiation of meaning." It's not just about picking up the words someone said, figuring out the dictionary equivalent of that expression and then saying or signing that. Interpreting involves the interpreter, speaker, and audience all working together to understand as a team. When the interpreter is far away from both the speaker and the audience, that kind of teamwork is harder.

Technical Requirements of RSI

This is all the more difficult given the technology requirements of RSI. The church and the interpreter both need fast enough internet connections and powerful enough computers to send and receive high-quality video and audio. Of those two, video is definitely the most demanding.

One platform recommends that everyone broadcasting, interpreting, or receiving the interpreting has a minimum internet connection speed of 10–15Mbps.[7] That might not seem like much but, in some rural areas and for people using smartphones to experience the interpreting, it can be a lot. To get such speeds on a smartphone would require a stable 4G or 5G connection. For spoken languages, people can receive just the audio, and can manage with 1Mbps. However, that still means that everyone listening to the interpreting inside the church needs that same connection speed, on top of the bandwidth needed to broadcast the service in the first place.

RSI also requires each interpreter to have a decently powerful PC or Mac running an up-to-date operating system, a USB headset (definitely not Bluetooth!) and a wired (Ethernet) connection to the internet.

---

5 Napier, "Interpreting Omissions," 117–42.
6 Eraslan, "International Knowledge Transfer," 75.
7 "FAQ for Technicians | Interactio."

Wi-Fi and Bluetooth are well known to be bad ideas for interpreters, due to connection quirks or brief dropouts, and smartphones are simply not powerful enough for the job.

Personally, I use a good quality USB microphone, separate USB headphones (including a backup set), a monitor in addition to my laptop screen, and an ergonomic keyboard and mouse, connected to a decently powerful, external fan-cooled laptop running a regularly updated copy of Windows 11. My setup is nowhere near the most elaborate or powerful among interpreters. RSI technology is much cheaper than traditional in-person simultaneous equipment, but it still has a noticeable cost.

If all this seems a little over the top, keep in mind that, in addition to the interpreting software, interpreters working in RSI for churches typically use a variety of other on-screen resources at the same time. A standard setup for me will include having the remote interpreting platform, a tab with Bible Gateway, several documents covering the sermon notes, the order of service, announcements and their associated terminology, a terminology website for looking up terms that come out of the blue, and a link to WhatsApp for communicating with other interpreters. I need my laptop to run smoothly with all that going on while still passing excellent quality sound down the internet to the people listening.

As useful as RSI is, churches might think that they don't necessarily need interpreting to happen simultaneously, at the same time as people are speaking. Might it be possible to provide interpreting remotely but without everything happening at the same time? The answer is yes but, for reasons I will now explain, that kind of remote interpreting is rarely, if ever, seen on Sundays.

Remote Consecutive Interpreting

This form of interpreting dates back to the first three-way phone systems in the 1970s and involves the speaker or signer and the interpreter taking turns to speak. Today, it is still used when people need telephone interpreting at a doctor's office or when having an interpreter-mediated phone call with someone who doesn't speak their language. Video Remote Interpreting, it's more technology-heavy counterpart, has existed for decades and is often used in medical and legal settings—especially for sign language interpreting.

That it is most commonly used for meetings involving conversations might tell us something about why it isn't used in church. While it would be possible for the interpreter and preacher to switch over with each sentence using this method, and it might even be possible for the interpreter to take notes and listen to longer stretches of the sermon at a time, I have never seen this happen. Remote interpreting always introduces some kind of delay. This might end up going unnoticed in a conversation and even when it is used to deliver simultaneous interpreting, but for use in Sunday services or large conferences, this delay would quickly mean that people lose their place and lose interest.

While it would be unusual and possibly unhelpful to see remote consecutive interpreting in a Sunday service, it might still have its uses. Many of the same technologies that make RSI possible can be repurposed for remote consecutive and there is no real reason why it couldn't be used in pastoral and marital counselling, home groups, Bible studies, and even leadership meetings.

If RSI is the world-shrinking, high-tech powerhouse of church interpreting that is perfectly at home with big stages and bright lights, remote consecutive, which I haven't even abbreviated, is the low-profile, well-used screwdriver that you use in the background, for jobs that aren't seen by the general public. While it isn't suitable for big stages and flashy conferences, most of church life happens between Sunday services. Remote consecutive can help most in these in-between moments and meetings. It is remote interpreting for the small meetings and deep discussions that leave a lasting impression, precisely because they are not for the whole world to see. But what if the interpreters are there with you in the building?

In-Person Simultaneous Interpreting (Sim)

In-person simultaneous interpreting is possibly the most famous form of interpreting. You might recognize it from the UN, NATO, the European Union, big Christian conferences, and just about every film involving interpreters. It looks complicated. It seems expensive and yet it is still usable in many churches. How does it work and what does it take to set it up?

As the name suggests, and as was mentioned earlier, it means that the interpreters speak or sign while the original speaker is speaking or signing. What that looks like depends on a big decision: what technology does the church want to use, if any?

For spoken languages and on the side of using no technology at all is a form of in-person simultaneous (henceforth just "sim") where the interpreter simply whispers their interpreting directly into people's ears. Often called whispered interpreting or referred to using its French translation, *chuchotage*, this is the kind of interpreting I described in chapter 7.

Whispered Interpreting

Whispered interpreting is cheap, relatively flexible, and requires no set up. If it is needed in more languages, churches can simply add interpreters. If it is needed for more people than can reasonably hear the same whisper at the same time, the church can just add interpreters. If it isn't needed one week, there is no expensive kit to put away and no room taken up by devices no one is using. It sounds like it might be perfect for churches. Why might it not be?

Well, for a start, whispered interpreting isn't as flexible as it might seem. There are hard limits as to how many people can listen to an interpreter whisper at the same time. Whispered interpreting works fine for very small, quiet groups of say three to five people. Above that and the interpreter isn't so much whispering as talking at roughly the same volume as they would normally. To put this in perspective, I have six children (not all of whom are quiet) so my family is already above the limit for whispered interpreting.

Even with the perfect number of people, whispered interpreting still has a problem. It is very disturbing. Every time I have offered whispered interpreting for any length of time, I have had at least one person asking me to be quiet. For people nearby, it easily distracts them from the service. For the people who need the interpreting, it means that they will always hear two voices, and might feel separated from everything that is going on. It often means that people are stuck in uncomfortable positions, leaning in to hear the interpreter. It is also unfeasible in noisy churches, conferences, or anywhere with music.

Personally, I would prefer to strike it completely off the list of interpreting modes used in churches, but I know that isn't reasonable. What I *will* say is that it needs to be used carefully, in smaller gatherings and almost certainly needs to be acknowledged from the front. People need to know that there is a good reason for the disturbance, and that the interpreter isn't just so bored, they are telling stories all through the service.

Churches also need to consider how to minimize disruption for those who don't need interpreting, without separating the people who need it from the rest of the congregation. Putting those who need interpreting in their own little corner might seem like a good idea, but corners we create during the service can lead to divisions and exclusion afterwards. It certainly does not symbolize Christian unity across cultures and languages.

Sim with Technology

The limits with whispered interpreting and its problems lead some churches and most big conferences to adopt a different solution. Churches and Christian conferences can both offer sim using some kind of technology. This could be professional interpreting consoles linked to infrared receivers, a special kind of radio mic linked to radio receivers, or a remote interpreting platform in the church itself that people connect to using their own devices.

No matter the exact technology used, they share one thing in common. In this form of sim, the interpreters sit in soundproof booths or, where they are lacking, a room nearby, and provide their interpreting from there. This interpreting is then broadcast somehow to those who need it. The advantages of offering interpreting this way are numerous.

For a start, the quality of the sound sent to the interpreters and therefore the results of their work and their long-term mental and physical health, are much better. Soundproof booths or isolated rooms all but eliminate background noise and allow interpreters to get on with their work in peace.

This form of interpreting is also much more peaceful for those who don't need the interpreting and those who need the interpreting alike. Those who need the interpreting don't need to worry about the strange effects of background noise, nor do they need to worry about leaning into uncomfortable positions to listen into the interpreters. Those who don't need the interpreting don't even need to realize it exists, as the interpreting goes on in the background without them hearing anything about it.

This also means that the service itself can largely go on as if the interpreting didn't exist. The preaching, praying, music and announcements can all go on as they did before, more or less. The service will be the same length as it has always been, without any interruption and without any whispering in the background.

So if this form of sim is so useful, why is it still quite rare? The most obvious reason is that it is expensive. Professional interpreting booths, consoles, and receivers can easily set churches back tens of thousands of dollars. This puts such equipment beyond the reach of all but the very biggest churches and the most well-funded conferences. Cheaper solutions are possible but the cost savings are not always worthwhile, given the compromises.

The decision to use this form of interpreting without using the most expensive equipment often leads to unintended consequences. The use of remote interpreting platforms obviously has its own costs. Cheaper alternatives such as video conferencing software isn't necessarily a perfect answer. Each church has to decide whether it is desirable or helpful or even possible to ask everyone who wants to listen to the interpreting to bring their own internet enabled device. In addition, unless the church is willing to provide its own high bandwidth Wi-Fi connection, they are also asking people to bring their own internet connection. In short, moving from traditional interpreting equipment to internet-enabled equivalents simply transfers the cost from the church on to those receiving the interpreting, which may or may not be reasonable.

Using remote interpreting platforms will also incur a cost to the church. In addition to things like licenses, which may be paid on an annual or monthly basis, churches will also have to pay the cost of the equipment that the interpreters use—such as laptops or computers of some kind that meet the basic requirements of the platform. These requirements change fairly regularly, so churches will need to make sure that this equipment is kept up to date and is suitable for the task. Churches will also need to supply good quality headsets and microphones. Each of these also has a cost.

There is no way to provide sim for spoken languages without some kind of cost. It could be the cost of disturbing people during whispered interpreting or the cost of some kind of technology for every other type of sim. Yet these costs create a place where everyone experiences the church service in their own language at the same time. In the case of some forms of technologically enabled sim, the church can also use the exact same technologies to make their services accessible to people around the world who speak different languages. When churches use some kind of remote interpreting platform or video conferencing software, the ability to reach anyone in the world who has an internet connection comes for free.

Sign Language Interpreting

When it comes to sign language interpreting, things become more straightforward. Sign language interpreting doesn't require the soundproof booths of spoken language sim. For interpreting into a sign language, the interpreter needs to be able to hear the speaker, and the people requiring the interpreter need to be able to see the interpreter. This can be done in various ways. In smaller churches, this could be achieved simply by having the interpreter stand in front of the congregation. As long as the interpreter can clearly see and hear the speaker, this will be just fine. Larger churches may look to use video feeds for people to see the interpreter, alongside sound and video monitoring for the interpreter to see and hear the speaker. There are various ways to have the interpreters on screen for those who need them, which can be discussed with sign language specialists at the time of the event.

For interpreting from a sign language into a spoken language, often called voicing, things are slightly different. In this case, the interpreter needs an absolutely clear view of the signer and any visual aids, slides, or pictures they may be using. It is vital that the interpreter has an unimpeded clear view, even more so than it is for the congregation to have one. Depending on how many people need to hear the interpreters, the headsets used in spoken language sim can be used, or the interpreter can just speak into a microphone. Again, the specifics of this setup need to be discussed with an expert. It's quite easy to miss something which seems obvious to an expert but isn't at all obvious to someone who doesn't usually work with interpreters.

In both cases, sign language interpreting may share some of the distracting effects of whispered interpreting. These are heightened in the case of voicing. In the case of interpreting into a sign language, those who don't require the interpreting can simply choose not to look at the interpreter.

A Summary of Sim

Setting up various forms of sim is more complicated than any form of RSI. The very fact that the interpreters are in the room or close by means that we need to plan ahead. One of the bonuses of RSI is that, since it piggybacks onto the church's existing sound and video setup, the technical complexities are already dealt with.

Yet the advantage of having interpreting in the room is that the interpreters are better able to adjust their work to the needs of the situation. Being in the room or close enough means they can see, even if just by the backs of people's heads, whether the interpreting is working well. In addition, being in the same place as the meeting is taking place allows interpreters to discuss with people what they got from the service. This is especially useful in cases where the interpreting is going to be repeated, such as for several meetings during the same conference, or simply week after week in the same church.

In person sim shares with RSI the need to plan ahead to make sure that the interpreting will work. It's still remarkably easy for people to forget that interpreters are there. The demands of any form of simultaneous interpreting require special partnership between those who are speaking or signing and those who are interpreting them. The requirement to choose carefully where the interpreters sit or stand or which kind of equipment they will use simply reminds us of the care that we need to take when simultaneous interpreting is used.

All forms of simultaneous interpreting have incredible benefits. Yet all forms of simultaneous interpreting are, in one way or another, very demanding.

In-person simultaneous interpreting can be scalable. We can simply add interpreters or equipment as the language needs of the church grow. The cost of this will depend entirely on the equipment the church is using. Yet some churches might feel, looking at the technical difficulties and cost of sim, that a simpler option is required. Are there options that churches can use where interpreting into only one or two languages are required? The answer is yes. It is to this option that we will now turn.

In-person Consecutive Interpreting

This is the mode that many people associate with church interpreting. In fact, it was the very first interpreting mode I saw and the first I delivered. In the form of in-person consecutive interpreting most used in churches, the speaker or signer and the interpreter take turns. The preacher might say or sign a sentence and then the interpreter gives their version. Most often, both people are on stage together, in front of everyone watching.

Done well, this mode, which we will call "on-stage consec," is a demonstration of the priority God gives to the diversity of languages in our world. The speaker or signer and the interpreter work together in glorious harmony, illustrating by their teamwork just how good and pleasant it is when users of different languages dwell in unity.

Done badly, on-stage consec is an exercise in drawn out boredom. The two people speak or sign over each other, leading to confusion. Everything takes twice as long and feels even longer. People get grumpy, disorganized, or simply distracted.

Delivering on-stage consec well is a skill anyone can learn. Understanding how to deliver great on-stage consec begins with understanding how it works, alongside its advantages and disadvantages. Let's start with how it works.

How on-Stage Consec Works

On the surface, it seems simple enough. We can imagine on-stage consec during a sermon as the preacher saying or signing something and the interpreter giving their version. Then the preacher starts again and the

Implementation—The How and Who

interpreter takes their turn. On and on that goes until the end of the sermon. Simple, right?

Not quite. The most obvious question is "how much should the preacher say or sign before stopping?" This can get tricky because many preachers, especially those from more charismatic backgrounds, are used to splitting up what they say into sections of various sizes to emphasize points. Something like "GOD ... LOVES ... YOU" or "The Spirit ... and the bride ... say ... come" makes perfect sense in English but can become impossible to interpret in languages where the word order is different. In French, for example, "God loves you" becomes *Dieu t'aime* or *Dieu vous aime*, depending on whether the interpreter wants to make it sound like God is speaking to an individual or to an entire audience. In both cases, the word order is actually "God – you – loves." The object—the person or thing God loves—comes before the verb.

This is just one well-known issue that exists in interpreting between two languages that have been in contact for hundreds of years. Similar issues can become even more complex when it comes to interpreting between languages that are even more distant or between a spoken and a sign language, since sign languages are grammatically different than the spoken languages used in the same places.

While grammar can make short segments impossible to interpret, long segments are equally difficult unless the interpreter is specifically trained. If someone says or signs too much, the interpreter will likely forget parts of what was said and they will certainly miss out on conveying the proper emphasis, unless they have that special training I mentioned.

So how long should segments be? The answer lies between the two extremes. The exact length will change throughout the sermon and will depend on the skill of the interpreter and whether they have access to the sermon notes ahead of time. A very good starting point would simply be to stop at the end of every sentence. Each sentence should have, at the very least, a subject (the person or thing doing the action), a verb (the action), and an object (the thing the action is being done to). This means that "you shall love the Lord your God with all your heart, and with all your soul, and with all your mind, and with all your strength" (Mark 12:30, NRSV) is fine. Cutting that into "you shall love ... the Lord you God with all your ... heart, and with all your ... soul, and with all your ... mind, and with all your ... strength" would not be so helpful, especially when being interpreted into languages like Finnish, where the word for "with" comes much later in the sentence than in English.

In my experience, on-stage consec is much easier to follow if the speaker and interpreter get into a consistent rhythm and only break it for specific effect. This takes time to learn and often comes from practice and through having the humility to see the interpreter as a partner, or "co-preacher" as some have called the role of the interpreter in church.[8]

This level of partnership points to the advantages of on-stage consec. As well as being technologically simple to set up, it puts languages front and center in the church. This not only honors those who speak different languages but demonstrates to the whole church that languages are valued. Since there is no need for any extra equipment, apart from, at most, a spare microphone and a place for the interpreter to put their Bible, on-stage consec is also incredibly cheap.

Yet this low monetary price comes with other costs. On-stage consec will make everything longer. Additionally, for spoken languages at least, on-stage consec is frustratingly inflexible. Using it for interpreting into one language is easy. Into two languages and the church will need a sound technician who knows how to send the sound from different microphones to different loudspeakers. Three or more languages is simply not feasible.

There is another form of in-person consecutive interpreting, which is rarely seen in church. For professional conference interpreters, consecutive interpreting usually means taking notes on entire speeches using special note-taking techniques, and then delivering the entire speech once the speaker has finished. I have never seen this mode in church and doubt it would work, but the techniques required are useful for all church interpreters. They are especially useful when working with that special breed of preacher who tends to forget that they have an interpreter standing alongside them!

But Who Is Going to Do It?

Each interpreting option has pros and cons, but churches looking at them probably have a much more pressing question in mind: who is going to do the interpreting? Here there are three main options: use an automated interpreting app, use volunteers from the church, or use professionals. Let's look at each of these in turn.

Using Automated Interpreting Apps

Some of the drawbacks of using machine interpreting apps were discussed in chapter 6, but these apps do have several advantages. For one, they are almost always much cheaper than human interpreters. Next, people

---
8 Karlik, "Interpreter-Mediated Scriptures," 160–85.

can use them on their own devices, so there is no need for the church to even know which language someone speaks. Finally, these apps are always available and don't have the issues with fatigue, holidays, or stress that a human interpreter might have.

Yet the disadvantages still matter. For them to work, such apps usually need conditions with very little background noise. They will also always reflect the data that is put into them. For publicly available systems, that probably means data from large corpora (collections of texts), from intergovernmental organizations, or from linguistics research. While Bible translations do often figure in these datasets, everyday church vocabulary and especially vocabulary specific to certain denominations will not.

As I mentioned in chapter 6, this means that machine interpreting into French tends to lean towards Roman Catholic terms. Other languages tend to have similar internal biases towards whichever denominations, groups, and even religions are most common where those languages are spoken. Additionally, the continued use of the cascade model in most automated speech translation apps means that they cannot reflect any emotion at all. They produce flat, computer-generated voices. To see what that sounds like, type this French phrase into any online translator app and find the button to read the result aloud: *Est-ce que vous entendez l'enthousiasme dans ma voix?*

The result isn't horrible, but it sounds far from what we might expect from a human speaker. Imagine hearing that voice for the length of an entire church service. Would it help you to be pulled into the sermon or would it sound like another wearying interaction with one of those automated telephone menus that companies put in place to make it harder to talk to an actual human being? Would you like to hear this voice Sunday after Sunday?

We have not even begun to ask serious theological questions. There are important questions to be asked about whether computers can preach sermons and what that means for relying on them to interpret sermons. It is important to put our use of machine interpreting apps in the context of our theology of what it means to minister to migrants and disciple people in different languages. Cost will always be an issue but we cannot ignore the fact that the language provisions we offer also reflect theological views and priorities.

Beyond all the technical restrictions and theological issues, it is important to ask again what using machine interpreting apps really says about our heart for people who speak different languages. We know for sure that those apps aren't perfect and we know for sure that the resulting sound is not as natural as it could be. We know for sure that we are providing, at best, an imperfect solution. Yet that is what we continue to offer.

Imagine coming to church and being told that people from another country would receive comfortable seats, complimentary tea, coffee, and biscuits afterwards while people like you would be asked to sit on the floor at the back and would be shuttled out the back door when the service finished? Imagine going to a church where rich people were given the best seats and poor people were sent to go sit somewhere uncomfortable (Jas 2:1–8).

When we choose to offer a deliberately lesser solution to people when better options are available then we are showing partiality—creating church services where one group has an entirely different experience than another. The question should not be "how can we do this multilingual church thing with as little effort as possible?" but "how do we do our best to ensure that everyone in this meeting has as similar an experience as possible?" or "which barriers do we need to break down so that we aren't showing partiality or favoritism?"

There are, of course, situations where relying on machine interpreting is the only or best option. Where the language makeup of a church changes suddenly or from week to week, then it might be impossible to get human interpreters at short notice. Where a church doesn't have access to interpreters or lacks the budget to make up for any gaps in what the church can provide in-house, then machine interpreting will be better than none at all.

But machine interpreting should not be seen as a free and easy solution, nor as a viable long-term option. Apps can plug gaps and are useful for those welcoming people to church, for relaxed conversations over tea and coffee, and for some use elsewhere. When what is said isn't of great importance, or where tone of voice and artificiality don't really matter, machine interpreting apps have their place. But they do not replace human interpreters or make them less necessary. They are not a perfect solution for delivering multilingual church. They are a helpful tool but need to be used with caution and only when, for whatever reason, human interpreters or working in another language are not suitable.

Using Interpreters from within the Church

This solution is by far the most common when churches are looking to deal with language differences. A church will identify which members use both languages, familiarize them with the relevant technology and launch them into interpreting.

Implementation—The How and Who

Training on church interpreting is rare, so most church interpreters will have a similar experience to mine. One day I had a short trial of my interpreting skills during a youth service; two days later I was at an international youth conference, interpreting on stage in front of a couple of hundred young people from three countries.

Don't get me wrong: there are definite advantages to using people from within the church. They tend to know and understand the words people usually use. They will tend to be known and trusted. Some might even already have leadership responsibilities or experience in preaching.

Interpreters from inside the church also tend to share the church's values. This means that church leaders can often trust that the interpreters will interpret with their hearts and not just their heads.[9] This practice is especially important given how often leaders, preachers, and interpreters in church have discussed the need to interpret with the whole self.[10] In fact, it seems like the more important interpreting is to a church, the more churches look for interpreters who will act as partners, not just as language machines.[11]

Further, it almost goes without saying that volunteers from inside the church will be considerably less expensive than professionals from outside the church. This fact often goes unsaid as few churches would want to publicly announce that cost was a deciding factor in how they provided interpreting. However, in many cases, it is.

For churches without large budgets, using volunteers from within the church makes financial sense and may be the only reasonable option. It is not a sin to admit that budgets are stretched, and they will not be able to cover the weighty fees charged by professionals.

With all this in mind, why would any church do anything other than enlist the services of volunteer church members if they are looking to provide interpreting? To answer that, it helps to think through the process of working with interpreters.

The Disadvantages of Volunteer Interpreters

For a start, how do churches find suitable volunteers? Few people have experience in testing the competence of interpreters and fewer churches have experience telling good interpreters from bad ones. Assuming that there is someone in the church that speaks both languages well enough, it is entirely possible that they will still lack what it takes to interpret.

---

9   Balci Tison, "Interpreter's Involvement," 122–23.
10 Hokkanen, "Experiencing the Interpreter's"; Hild, "Role and Self-Regulation," 177–94; Harkness "Transducing a Sermon," 112–42.
11 Downie, "Stakeholder Expectations," 171–72.

During my training as a professional interpreter, it was very clear from early on who was happy in the interpreting booth and who was unsuited and desperate to never see one again. Not all bilinguals make competent interpreters.

Interpreting is very demanding in terms of attention and alertness. Trained, experienced professionals performing sim will generally alternate with a partner every twenty to thirty minutes to avoid lapses and ensure that the quality of the interpreting remains high. If that is the standard for professionals, how long should volunteer interpreters work before a break?

Even if a church finds willing interpreters, figuring out if they are any good is another question entirely and monitoring their work can easily become an afterthought. A lack of oversight can lead to real difficulties, even church splits. Interpreters could easily adapt what is said to match what they think *should* have been said. How can anyone know if a volunteer is providing a good standard of interpreting?

Things get even more difficult when it comes to training. Only a few places in the world offer training to church interpreters. Further, interpreter training courses tend to be aimed either at those looking to work with the EU, UN, or NATO, or court and medical interpreters. This tailored focus affects the skills taught and the pricing. While it is possible for churches to train interpreters, doing so would require the church to have people with experience in interpreting and in teaching interpreters. While there are helpful books on interpreting, these primarily demonstrate that interpreting requires much more than just knowing how to translate one word at a time from one language to another. In fact, interpreting really doesn't require that at all.

It is possible for a church to offer useful training for interpreters. A small, but growing, community of church interpreters have completed professional training and can help churches. Providing skills training is possible, but it requires calling in expert help.

Ensuring that the volunteer interpreters get the ongoing support they need and that their work is integrated into church life (see chapter 13) requires expert support. Like initial training, ongoing support is something that few churches are used to providing. But such training matters. In fact, if a church is to avoid language provision simply being another ministry or project that gets shoved into a corner, ongoing support and integrating language provision into the practice of the church life are essential.

Using Professional Interpreters

The final possibility is the most expensive. If you know where to find them, there are professional interpreters who can do church work well.

Quite a few Christians can be found in the professional interpreting world, and many of them can deliver when churches need it most.

On the surface, this takes away most of the challenges churches face when they use volunteers from within the church. When you use professionals, you don't have to worry about providing training. Ongoing support is still important, but quality checking is not going to be quite as difficult. In fact, since professional interpreters most often work in teams of two, they end up checking each other's quality.

Using professional interpreters who are familiar with church interpreting also means that you get the terminology for free. These people might not yet know the exact words used in your church but they will have been trained on how to prepare for an assignment and will be up to speed within hours. Within a few services, they can start sounding like people who have been in your church all their lives. Christian professionals also come with the tendency to interpret with their whole selves, just like churches would expect from volunteers.

Of course, professional interpreting isn't perfect. The biggest barrier is simply cost. It is quite foolish to put exact prices here as they will be different in each area and will change over time. However, I would be surprised if any church in Europe or North America could get professional interpreting for less than six hundred dollars per language, per service. Paying for any interpreting equipment and platforms can add to this considerably. This puts professional interpreting out of reach of all but the largest churches.

A more affordable option, however, is inviting professionals to offer training for interpreters and preachers on how to deliver interpreting well in churches. These courses can be shared among a few churches to cut costs further and can help to gradually give churches the best of both worlds. While a single course will not take volunteers from novices to experts, having professionals on-hand to offer support can make a big difference. For larger churches, using professionals can be worth it, if for no other reason than to reduce the staff and volunteer time needed. For smaller churches, getting advice and training from professionals can help the church get the best out of what it can offer.

Is There a Perfect Option?

It might seem strange to read a chapter as long as this one without arriving at a perfect option. As a consultant church interpreter, I share that frustration. I would dearly like to simply say "the research says to do it like this" or "the Bible says to do it like that." But I have become very familiar with the complications that make a perfect solution in one church utterly unsuitable for another.

At the most basic level, I would say that bringing different languages into the church service and working to dethrone your locally dominant language are both fundamentally important. Showing every week that you value the different languages represented in your church, making space for voices that might go unheard, and being careful to ensure that everyone receives a similar experience are baseline commitments.

What that looks like in your church will be for you to decide. Do you need to take another look at services in different languages? If you do, when and how will you bring everyone together? Might it be worth having multilingual Sunday services but monolingual Bible studies or home groups? Is it worth looking at what machine interpreting can do? What about written translation?

What about interpreting? Is there the budget for some use of professionals? Are there volunteers ready and willing to do the work? Is it better for the interpreters to be in the church building or working remotely? Should they work consecutively or simultaneously?

The answers to these questions will depend on your church's vision, strategy, resources, and needs. Treat this chapter as a guide to what's on offer, like the menu of a restaurant. Not everyone wants to grab the steak. Some people need a vegetarian option. Others just want a pizza. Whatever your needs, resources, and vision, there is a solution that is just right for your church.

In addition to considering costs, I would strongly advise churches to look at these options through the lens of theology and the gospel. Churches absolutely should seriously consider the theological implications of having a dominant language or using machine interpreting. Leaders should also be aware that the solutions they choose speak volumes to everyone in the church, even before any word is spoken or signed in another language. These decisions matter.

I want to end this chapter by re-emphasizing that whichever solution or solutions you choose, they will not and cannot work without clear vision and careful strategy. In my training webinars, I am fond of saying "strategy before mechanics." This chapter has given an overview of the different possible mechanics of creating multilingual church. Even this is just scratching the surface. None of it works without the power and love of God, vision, strategy, planning, prayer and, as the next chapter will discuss, careful and deliberate maintenance.

CHAPTER 13

Maintenance—The Future

The Baby Needs to Be Fed and Changed

Anyone who has had a child will recognize the feeling. There is a period of intense preparation, financial investment, thinking, planning, reading, and then, all at once, you are a parent! I remember my dad talking about the shock of bringing his first child (my brother) home from the hospital for the first time. The shock didn't quite hit me like that, especially as our oldest needed a few days in the hospital to gain a bit of weight before he could come home.

For me, the biggest reality hit was when I was carrying our baby son down the stairs and my foot missed a step causing me to fall down the rest. Without even thinking about it, my body flipped me onto my back and held tightly to the baby. He was fine—it must have felt like going down a slide on a cushion to him. I was the one nursing bruises. From then on, I knew that my reactions would be different, my decision making would be different, and my priorities would be different.

Responsible parents know that having a baby is just the start. The baby needs to be fed and changed and protected and taught and parented. We could say something similar about having a pet, or buying a car, or even—now that regular updates and security precautions are a part of everyday life—buying a computer. Having the baby, or the pet, or the car, or the computer is not the end. It's just the beginning.

Offering language provision in a church is surprisingly similar. It doesn't particularly matter whether it's a translated website, bought-in written materials, or some kind of interpreting. Having the provision there is just the start. The baby needs to be fed and changed and protected. Whatever you are doing towards multilingual church needs to be maintained and checked and evaluated and improved. So what does that look and feel like? The best way I can describe it is with a different analogy.

Having the provision there is just the start.

Is This Thing On?

For what seemed like an eternity, I was the main sound technician in that church in the west of Scotland that I mentioned in chapters 1 and 7. For a good chunk of that period, we didn't have our own building. At the end of each service, most of the equipment was packed into a heavy wooden box, with the sound desk on top and a long, heavy, multi-core cable underneath. Various drawers held microphones and cables and square nine-volt batteries.

After wiring everything up, a job which seemed to get longer every week, I went through the careful task of testing everything. Every microphone was checked. Every battery was tested. I hit a few keys on the keyboard and asked a guitarist to play a chord or two. I knew that you couldn't have good sound unless everything was connected, with no broken cables or dead batteries. More often than not, something needed attention. Maybe a loudspeaker cable was getting loose, a plug wasn't in the wall fully, or a battery was dead. Since I wired everything up, I knew exactly how to follow the wiring, locate the fault, and fix the issue.

Language provision works in a similar way. At regular intervals, someone needs to go through every stage and make sure it works. Is it producing something people understand and can use? Are there any misunderstandings? Is everyone working together well? Does all the equipment still work? Is anyone burning out or overworking? Are there sufficient backup volunteers? What does the training pipeline look like? What needs to be tweaked or removed or improved?

Building feedback loops, where everyone feels free to share how they are experiencing the language provision, is vital for any church or Christian organization. It's one thing to check that people are understanding the translation or interpreting, or that they are enjoying the services in their language. It is quite another to check with the leaders of those services or the interpreters and translators to see whether they feel empowered and enabled to deliver their best work. Being humble enough to learn where the senior church leadership could do better is an even higher level of accountability and most likely is the one where the biggest changes can happen.

Honestly, there is very little research on maintaining language provision. Researchers tend to arrive somewhere, do a case study over a few days, weeks, or months and then return to their offices to analyze the data. But there are some useful insights we can learn from elsewhere and that a professional interpreter could tell you.

Back in chapters 1 and 9, I mentioned CLW, the church in Germany that I came across when I visited the lady who would become my wife. I also mentioned that I studied that church for my PhD and learned a lot about the importance of language provision being woven throughout the life of a church, rather than being an isolated ministry. If I needed proof of what could happen when language provision is an afterthought, I got it in the other church I studied.

I changed the name of this second church to IEN for a variety of reasons. IEN was and remains an international church grouping that likes to put on big, loud, punchy conferences. I studied two of these. At both conferences, the language provision looked to be excellent. The interpreting booths rivalled any I have seen as a professional. The receiving equipment was of a high standard and the interpreters were, for the most part, experienced. They knew what they were doing. Those listening knew what to expect and had strong opinions on what they wanted.

There were just a few glitches. When I visited, the church as a whole had a fairly negative view of language. Interpreting was there because it had to be, since there were several people who didn't speak English. Interviews with those listening to the interpreters and observations of the preaching found that, in this church group, people saw interpreters as equivalent to a microphone or a piece of equipment. Their work and its challenges were minimized, and many believed that anyone with the requisite language skills was fine to do the job, as long as they knew how to do it without letting their own views or ideas get in the way.

Those views were reflected in practice. Important parts of the conference happened in places the interpreters couldn't see. Lone interpreters worked for entire services without a break. There was no record of interpreter support or of any communication between the speakers and interpreters.[1] The only real quality checks involved someone knowing the interpreter and people occasionally correcting terminology they thought was wrong.

It made sense then that interpreting in this group of churches was almost entirely restricted to the big conferences and the set piece events. In fact, I found out from much later conversations that, for some events, it simply wasn't available at all and people had to muddle along.

If language provision is to go from a few one-off moments to being part of the church, it cannot be an afterthought. Like any part of the church, it needs regular attention, godly evaluation, and pastoral care. In fact, pastoral care is so important, it is worth discussing it on its own.

Interpreting Sometimes Hurts

My most traumatic interpreting assignments were for churches.

The first was during a fundraiser for a people group who were subject to such discrimination that their only economic activity was selling their own women and children into prostitution. The second was during a church group's consultation on their migration policy, where I interpreted the effects of epidemics and war on the family of one pastor.

---
1 Downie, "Stakeholder Expectations," 127.

Over the past five years or so, people have started talking about the mental and emotional stresses of working as an interpreter. Community and public service interpreters have discussed the tensions of interpreting cases of abuse, violence, and persecution. Medical interpreters have talked about interpreting diagnoses that someone would not recover. Sign language interpreters started understanding the importance of professional supervision, a service that allows them to work through their emotional reactions and ethical decision-making.[2]

Eventually, interpreters of all kinds have started getting comfortable discussing mental health and vicarious trauma. The latter occurs when people experience lingering emotional effects from empathizing with those who have recounted their own trauma. A turning point for me was the episode of the *Troublesome Terps* podcast, where we interviewed Justine Mason, a senior lecturer in mental health nursing.[3] Suddenly, it was fine to confess to the tough emotions that interpreting stirs up, even in safe-looking conference and church interpreting.

What does all this have to do with church interpreting?

If your church ever has sermons on emotionally difficult subjects or openly speaks about recovery from abuse, addiction, witchcraft, or violence, then anyone involved in language provision is at risk of vicarious trauma. If the work of those providing language services involves having to write, speak, or sign emotionally impactful content in another language, it stands to reason that they are at even higher risk. This means that any church covering these topics even occasionally needs to take responsibility for providing adequate professional trauma support for everyone involved. This support should be in addition to the regular member care that anyone working in or around churches will require.

Additionally, keep in mind that translation and interpreting are both cognitively difficult, if for different reasons. This difficulty is compounded if people are trying to do the work without prior training. Professional interpreters and translators have a whole range of techniques, skills, and resources to manage the demands of their work. They might also be part of supportive communities who can offer practical help and, in the best case, emotional support. Volunteer translators and interpreters almost certainly do not have these techniques or skills available. They will need extra help.

If churches want to be able to remain multilingual over the long-term, everyone involved in the mechanics of offering language provision needs access to some kind of member care. In church interpreting research, it is

---

[2] Darroch and Dempsey, "Interpreter's Experiences."

[3] Downie, Drechsel, and Gansmeier, "Mental Health for Interpreters."

common to see interpreters called "co-preachers."[4] If a church is aware of the care and support that pastors and leaders need, they should offer the same level of support to anyone involved in multilingual ministry. They stand at the sharp end of the church's ministry of reconciliation and often pay the price for it. That price must be taken seriously. Leaders of multilingual churches also stand at the sharp end since being multilingual often requires deeper changes and harder work than the church might expect.

Change before You Have To

If we honestly examine what it takes to maintain a multilingual church, it looks like hard work. It *is* hard work. Mario Wahnschaffe's book, *Building an International Church* testifies to the challenges and stresses but also to the joy and glory. Even as an experienced interpreter and researcher, I learned something important from that book: being a multilingual church means being a church that is willing to change. That change may come from providing new kinds of pastoral support, amplifying voices you might not otherwise hear, and even accepting people onto the senior leadership team who share nothing but the love of Christ with those already there.

These challenges should not be much of a surprise. Research on multiethnic church has shown that the make-up of the leadership team says a lot about how well the church will navigate the difficulties of being multiethnic.[5] We should expect a similar effect in multilingual churches. Trying to be a multilingual church with a monolingual leadership team is eventually self-defeating.

Like it or not, the languages we speak and the cultures we belong to affect the way we think and how we approach decisions. Assuming that speakers of the locally dominant language are the people best placed to make decisions about language provision for everyone else seems ironic, if not prideful.

Perhaps the best way to keep multilingual church working for the long-haul is to have the humility to realize that a single ethnic or linguistic group in the church cannot and should not dominate leadership. No one group has a monopoly on being right or on hearing the voice of God.

The goal of diverse leadership is absolutely not a license for tokenism or for picking someone simply because of the color of their skin or their language skills. That would be unbiblical and foolish. However, if a church is genuinely multilingual and is attracting people from lots of different

---

4 Karlik, "Interpreter-Mediated Scriptures," 167; Balci Tison, "Interpreter's Involvement," 128–29; compare with Vigouroux "Double-Mouthed Discourse," 361–62.

5 Edwards, "Multiethnic Church Movement."

backgrounds, that should create a natural, spiritually effective route for people from different backgrounds to exercise their God-given gifts.

Unless we really think that God only chooses leaders who speak certain languages, we need to question any situation where people from different language groups are not rising to leadership over time. What might be going wrong in the environment? What faulty definitions of leadership might we have? Why are people not being equipped and enabled to serve with the gifts God has given them?

I doubt that honest answers to these questions can come from a single ethnic or linguistic group. Humbly finding ways to ask these questions in a culturally acceptable way is vital.

If we want to see what happens when we don't ask such questions, there is a simple example. In my research for this book, I was inspired by the story of a church in the USA that deliberately moved from being entirely composed of one ethnic minority to reaching across ethnic boundaries. When the church was studied, they had a thriving ministry to several ethnic minorities and to the ethnic majority in their city.

I checked on them recently by visiting their website. Nowadays, their leadership is entirely composed of one ethnic minority and pictures of church services show that they are no longer the multiethnic church they used to be. I don't know the full story, but I do think that there is always a danger that any multiethnic or multilingual church can drift back to homogeneity if the hard work isn't done to grow and maintain a linguistically or ethnically diverse leadership team.

No church defaults to being multilingual. It takes real effort and intention, as well as the power of God, for a church to stay there. Having the humility to listen to others and make space for them, taking the time to ask tough questions about how the work is going, and learning to change as the work keeps going—none of that is easy. But, if churches in multilingual communities are to reach the people God has called them to and if Christian organizations are to remain multilingual, these difficulties are unavoidable. No one ever said this road was easy, but it is the one God is calling many churches around the world to walk.

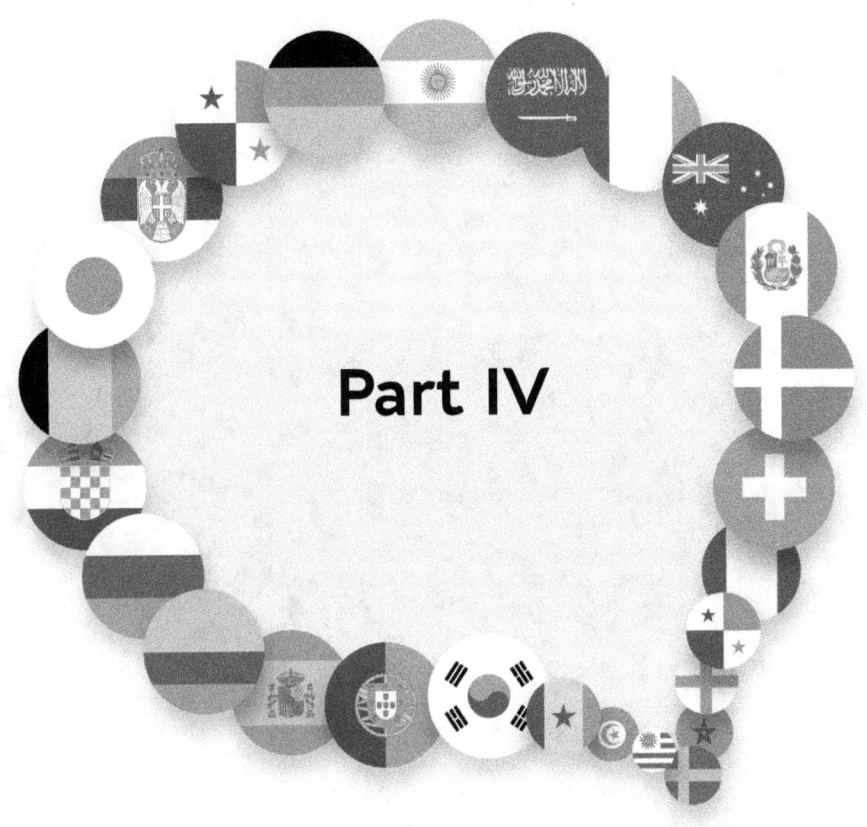

Part IV

Sunday Is Just the Start

CHAPTER 14

Excluding the Locals?

"We have to prioritize those already in the church." "What if people don't like eating food from other countries?" "It's best if people leave their previous identities at the door of the church. All that matters is that we are Christians together."

I have either heard or read the above phrases from church leaders or researchers on multiethnic church. They are all plausible positions. We can see why leaders would want to show the people already in the church that they come first and that everyone new will have to learn to settle in. We can imagine that people might not instantly love eating food from different countries, especially when they see it for the first time. We can also probably think of good verses to support the idea that national identities are far less important than spiritual ones.

All these statements are justifiable arguments, but they also show an emotion we might not want to admit: fear. Arguing that the people we already have must come first betrays a fear of losing people. Worrying about food betrays a fear of offence or a fear of the unfamiliar. As for asking people to leave their other identities outside tells us that somehow there is an intractable conflict between cultural and kingdom identities. If we are honest, it really means we want other people to become like us, since no one ever says lines like that to those who speak the locally dominant language or who conform to what we consider "normal."

> **We have to make sure that our legitimate concerns about resources, conflict, and loss are coming from the right place.**

My point is not that we should just leave those already in the church to get on with it. We can't abandon people. Yet, we have to make sure that our legitimate concerns about resources, conflict, and loss are coming from the right place. If we are carrying fear, especially fear of others, we need to confess it, bring it to God, and work with God and others to walk free of it. It is legitimate to be concerned about how those already in the church will react. It is not legitimate to use their concerns as a veil over racism or fear of others.

All Aboard!

My dad worked for our national railway for most of his adult life. I have ridden a lot of trains and heard a lot of stories about how things used to be. In old movies, there are often dramatic moments when people are about to board a train and a voice from off-screen shouts "all aboard!" to tell people that, if they don't get on now, the train will go without them. Even now, for long-distance trains in the UK, there are people called "train dispatchers" who check that everyone is on and then whistle and signal to the driver that all the doors are shut and they can pull away from the station. The driver needs to know that everyone is on board before they pull away.

Is everyone on board in your church? While I spent my teens in a tradition where it was accepted that leaders could just change the direction of the church at will, the reality is that nothing gets done just because leaders say it should. Especially with a change as fundamental as becoming multilingual, churches have to move as one and with the support of the congregation.

Vision casting is essential here, along with knowing the history and values of the church, and taking time to really listen to peoples' concerns. The reality is that everyone in the church has their own needs, passions, and desires. Showing people how leading the church towards being multilingual corresponds to these needs and desires, honestly admitting to the cost of change and the price of keeping things the same is always a work of biblical leadership.

Going back to our train metaphor, we would hardly expect anyone to get on a train if they had no idea where it was going. We have to know the direction and something about the route before we can agree to the journey.

Applying this metaphor of explaining the destination and the route to multilingual church takes a mixture of solid biblical preaching, covering the call to multilingualism covered in chapter 2, and the vision and strategy work from chapters 10 and 11. It is not enough to just say "we are going to become multilingual" or even to suddenly start with some kind of language provision. Leaders need to prayerfully work through conversations with people in the church, seek God, and then spend time carefully explaining where the church is heading, the reasons for the journey, and what the route might look like.

While this book has deliberately covered the challenges and technicalities of multilingual church, these are not the factors that will get people excited about the idea and inspire them to commit the time, resources, and money that multilingual church needs. Apart from the biggest interpreting nerds, no one is going to get excited about shiny interpreting booths or expensive remote interpreting platforms. Even fewer people are going to get excited about services in languages they don't speak. Some people might even find it strange to hear other languages used from the front of the church.

It is vital to preach and teach on how the gospel has broken racial, cultural, and language barriers and to explain that God's will was always for the kingdom of God to bring reconciliation. When people hear about racism being challenged, communities being united, and people worshipping God from every nation, tribe, and tongue in *their* church, something might just catch fire. We might want to call this heaven coming to earth. We might want to explain the relevance of our unity in Christ Jesus (Gal 3:28). We might want to dwell on the sheer breadth and power of all of Acts 2, from the believers gathering together in one place to them meeting house to house, now several thousand strong.

Yes, there is a price to pay. Yes, multilingual church is challenging. Yes, it is impossible without God. No responsible researcher or leader would ever try to ignore those realities. But multilingual church is breathtaking in its grandeur, scope, and relevance in our increasingly divided world. If the kingdom of God is the answer to the division and hatred people see around them, then multilingual churches in multicultural communities are signs that the kingdom of God is here. If we are declaring the full gospel in multicultural communities, it is hard to see any other biblical outcome.

Vision casting enables people to grasp the biblical vision of multilingual church and to understand how the history, resources, and vision of their church are leading it to its own specific way of becoming multilingual. It is worth repeating that the answers each church finds will be different. What a church of twenty thousand can do will differ from what a house church can manage. A new multilingual church plant will face different challenges and have different potential than an established church that is seeing its community change around it.

> **Vision casting is only the beginning.**

Excluded or Empowered?

Vision casting is only the beginning. Anyone can get people excited about a vision. It takes much more work and skill to help people see how the vision includes and needs their talents and skills. The goal is to help people realize that multilingual church isn't about preferring one group over another. It is about building churches where everyone is welcome and where everyone is reached, taught, and discipled, no matter which language they use.

This goal is all the more important since a common argument in many countries is that we can either accept migrants or look after the poor who share our skin color. Racism is most often pushed as a way of assuring the rights of the majority in the face of growing migrant populations.

Churches can demonstrate the lie of racism by embodying the truth that God's love is not limited by race, culture, or language. When everyone in the church feels at home and can use their gifts in some way, it becomes clear that reaching certain people does not mean excluding others.

But what does that really look like? Again, it will vary from church to church but it is worth asking what passions, skills, and talents people in the church have. While no single church can do every kind of outreach or ministry, God does not give people gifts to see them sit on the shelf. Perhaps God has gifted your church with people who are passionate about reaching people in retirement homes because that is where God is leading the church. Perhaps there are people waiting eagerly to create multilingual resources because that is God's vision for the church.

In multilingual church there is a place for everyone.

In addition, churches can encourage and equip people to use their gifts and talents in God-honoring, kingdom-building ways outside the walls of the church. Are there people God is calling into urban planning, poverty relief, business, or working with marginalized groups? If so, how can this work become part of the vision of the church, even if the work occurs in charities, the marketplace, or advocacy centers? The next chapter will cover more of this topic.

We need to expand our view of what ministry means and what multilingual church means. Instead of people from the dominant language and culture feeling threatened by multilingual church, the challenge is to help them see how the passions God has given them align with the vision of the church and how they can play their part. Even something as simple as being willing to learn how to cook a different cuisine or to serve tea and coffee can be a vital part of building churches where everyone is welcomed and feels at home.

Multilingual Church: Multi-Gifted Body

In multilingual church there is a place for everyone. That must include those from the dominant culture too. Where do monolinguals figure in your church's vision? We cannot afford to replace systems that put those from the dominant culture first with those that exclude them. This is true even though we will have to challenge the dominance of one culture or language. It remains true especially when difficult decisions around resources and ministries are being made.

This sounds theoretical because there are no fixed rules. There are, however, clear biblical guidelines. Paul's explanation of the church as a body (1 Cor 12) serves as a reminder of three important truths.

The first is that the point of gifts or roles is not to make us look good but for the good of the church (1 Cor 12:7). The church works best when the body works together. If God has given the church someone with a specific gift, it is a sign that he wants that gift used for the good of all. I remember being in a church where the leaders were happy for me to run the sound equipment or preach very occasionally but it was made clear several times that my language gifts were not deemed useful or helpful. The vision of the church might not have explicitly excluded those gifts but the reality of the church did.

Which gifts are going unused in your church? Where is there spiritual unemployment? Paul tells us that these spiritual gifts are for the good of all. He also reminds us that we belong together. Our church practices need to reflect that reality.

The second important truth is that each part of the body needs the others to function. No gift or place is sufficient on its own. An arm cannot claim superiority over the heart. The nose has no purpose apart from the head. A limb without a body dies quickly.

Each culture tends to elevate some gifts above others. It is true that Paul himself tells us to seek after the "greater gifts" (1 Cor 12:31, NIV) but this is not about seeking a higher position. The whole context of the passage and of course, the famous next chapter (1 Cor 13), should be enough to tell us that his "greater gifts" are the ones that allow us to serve more effectively. He is not telling us to seek after status or power, like the world does. Instead, we are to seek after gifts that allow us to love people more and minister more effectively as a body.

The third truth is that the core of Paul's comparison of the church to a body is the idea that we cannot afford to either look down on ourselves or mistreat others in the body. This understanding is important precisely because our gifts are given for the church and we cannot function properly without each other.

A multilingual church needs people who use the locally dominant language as much as it needs users of other languages. It needs those with expertise in interpreting, translation, multicultural ministry, or technology just as much as it needs those skilled in cleaning, administration, decoration, care, and finance. It needs worship leaders and worshippers, preachers and helpers, those who sow seed and those skilled in gathering.

If multilingual church is to be a place where everyone is welcome, we need to help the people already there to see how this is good news for them too. Yes, there will be times of discomfort. Yes, some practices will likely need to change. Yes, there is a price to pay. But taking the time to pray with people in the church, listen to their concerns, cast a compelling vision, and follow up by empowering people to use the gifts God has given them will surely help people see that this vision is for them too. Multilingual church is impossible without the power of God. It also happens to be something that God loves to build through his people, no matter which languages they use.

CHAPTER 15

Sunday Is Just the Start

It's all well and good to talk about multilingual church as a place where everyone feels welcome, as I did in the previous chapter, but what does that actually look like? If a church wants everyone to flourish with the skills and passions God has given them no matter which language they speak, it will take more than a few nice services every week.

Reading through this book may give the impression that the core of multilingual church can be found in Sunday services. That is certainly where church interpreting research has been concentrated. Discussions of multiethnic church also tend to concentrate on integrating different cultures into worship, some of which was discussed in chapter 5. Yet the story doesn't end with Sunday. A church can have the best Sunday services on the planet but people can still feel unwelcome. The preaching can be amazing but discipleship might not happen. A church can spend on the best translation and interpreting, the most beautiful multilingual liturgies, and the shiniest websites or web streams but that might not be enough. In fact, there are growing multilingual churches that seem remarkably basic in the technology they use, the methods they try, and the services they put on once a week. What other factors might contribute to making multilingual church effective?

Make It Part of Everyday Church Life

What successful multilingual churches do seem to have in common—from the churches studied by Jill Karlik in The Gambia[1] to the church in Turkey studied by Alev Balci Tison[2] that twice pivoted its language strategy—is that being multilingual is not just a gimmick for Sundays. Somehow, using different languages becomes part of the DNA of the church.

Likewise, in his book, *Building an International Church*, Pastor Mario Wahnschaffe takes the time to explain how the vision of being an international church permeated every activity, especially the core work of fellowship, worship, teaching, ministry, and evangelism.[3] For them, this meant having an interpreting ministry, fostering ethnically uniform home groups, creating various kinds of meetings where members and leaders

---

[1] Karlik, "Interpreter-Mediated Scriptures."
[2] Balci Tison "Interpreter's Involvement."
[3] Wahnschaffe, *Building an International*, 315.

from different backgrounds could get to know each other, thinking carefully through teaching, ensuring people from different backgrounds were empowered to minister, and being aware of the cultural nuances at play in international evangelism.[4]

Such wholesale changes rarely happen at once. It will take time for people to catch the vision to the extent that they are ready to apply it to their own work. It can be hard to accept that the habits and practices we are used to are simply not suitable as a church changes. What works for a church full of white Westerners who have gone to church all their lives and know instinctively when to sit, stand, kneel, and respond will feel awkward to people who are from a different background.

The irony is that a church often cannot know how to embed multilingualism throughout all its work until the leaders are willing to listen to the experiences of those who use other languages. This is very similar to recent conversations on how churches can welcome and empower those with various disabilities.[5] The seven recommendations that came from one recent study all focus on taking time to proactively seek out direct feedback from those with disabilities and those who work with them, listening to their point of view, being ready to make meaningful changes to the physical space, how it is used, and addressing any unhelpful attitudes people might have.

It takes very little imagination to see how this can be applied to multilingual church. A church might already have a rhythm of Bible study groups, prayer meetings, and member' meetings. Listening to those with a different cultural or linguistic background might mean trying new ways to conduct those meetings or even looking to meet needs that the church was not aware of. There might be a need for groups to promote racial reconciliation, or language learning, or simply to support people struggling with poverty, exclusion, or parenting.

Embedding multilingualism throughout a church means a lot more than ensuring that people can participate in a meeting in their language. It means rethinking how the church works and meets to best reach, teach, and disciple the community around it. Perhaps all that is needed is some kind of interpreting in home groups and pastoral support for interpreters. Or maybe the church finds itself looking to partner with local Christian counselling organizations to provide trauma support. It could simply be that the church bulletin needs to be translated or that one service a quarter should be held in another language, with English speakers needing to rely on the language provision offered by the church.

---

4 Wahnschaffe, 315–512.

5 Carter et al., "Addressing Accessibility," 1–22.

Once again, the mechanics are far less important than the strategy. This is especially the case since no church can do everything people might want it to. Resources are always going to be stretched, even if the main resource any church draws on is the people in it. Thinking strategically, based on open, honest dialogue is always the place to start.

What if This Were Me?

Imagine yourself as someone who doesn't speak the locally dominant language. How would you find the church? Where would you find service times and location? How would you find out what kind of church it was or which language provision was available?

Now imagine someone arriving at the church. You might imagine that a Sunday service would be their first contact with people in the church, but it might not be. Which outreach activities or groups attract people who speak different languages? How might they experience them if they don't use your locally dominant language?

When would they be in contact with the church throughout the week? What is their experience going to be like without the locally dominant language? Now think about your main Sunday services. What do they look like or feel like if you use a different language?

It is helpful to answer these questions yourself and then ask others to work through the process. Take note of the differences between those who use the locally dominant language and those who don't. Think through age group ministries, outreach activities, home groups, and any other point at which someone might come into contact with the church.

What does that journey look like? Where are the gaps in provision? Where does the journey end? How does it feel to be in your church but not speak the locally dominant language?

I know that some churches will baulk at doing this kind of exercise. It is remarkably easy to hide behind "God will take care of it" or "if God wants us to do it, he will lead us to." Sometimes God drops an idea into our spirits from nowhere and sometimes God puts the plough in our hands and asks us to start tilling the field.

Taking the time to carefully and lovingly walk through what it means to be someone without the locally dominant language in our churches is a way that we come alongside people. It's a way that we listen and gain wisdom. It's a way that we love God and love our neighbor. This is not some fancy corporate method, dreamed up by a marketing department. We show that we actually care by following the journeys that people take as they come in contact with our church, choose to find out more, and start to walk with us.

This is all part of how we live in "humility and gentleness, with patience, bearing with one another in love" (Eph 4:2b, NRSV). It takes humility to realize that the way we currently do church is actively turning some people off. It takes gentleness and patience to have the tough conversations and to keep listening well past the moment we think we already have the answer.

Often, how we do church becomes a reflection of who we are. There are some churches who are justifiably proud of not having changed their order of service much in hundreds of years. For them, it is a mark of honor that someone from the Victorian era could walk into the church and still recognize the hymns sung, the blessings spoken, and the way those involved in the service dress and move. There is great value in tradition.

There are other churches who value innovation. New lighting setups, multimedia, sermons that include discussion, inviting people to reflect or worship in new ways—these are all seen as part of meeting the needs of our modern communities. There is, of course, great value in singing a new song to the Lord and being all things to all people. Innovation has a place too.

Walking through the experiences of those who do not use the dominant language of the church is not about tradition or innovation. It need not even be about shifts in liturgy or changing worship styles. The very fact of taking the time to walk through someone else's experience can help us to reflect on the details, both large and small that position people to receive from God and which might be the difference in how two different people experience the same church.

To see this in action, let's take language out of consideration for a moment. What does it feel like to be a visitor in your church? As someone who had the wonderful opportunity to visit many different churches in my own country in my teens, that question has real resonance for me. There were churches where someone is hardly over the threshold and they have a warm welcome and sometimes even a mug filled with sweets. In other places, you could slip in and out and no one would even know you existed. Some churches felt to me like a bewildering system of standing, sitting, kneeling, and handshaking, to the point where I often didn't know if this was a sit-down bit, a stand-up bit, or a repeat-the-line bit. I have been to traditional churches where people realized that not everyone knew what was going on and I have been in less traditional churches where, if you didn't know what was happening, it was an overwhelming muddle. This applies to both Sunday services and mid-week meetings.

Without getting into the debates over whether churches should be seeker friendly (that phrase alone seems like an unhelpful buzzword by now), I do think that it pays to ask how a visitor might experience your church. Are they welcomed? Do they know what is happening now and what will happen next? What if they have children with special needs? What if *they* have special needs? What if you have a visitor with a wheelchair or one who is blind or deaf?

These questions go beyond Sunday services. The points where we realize that a visitor would feel out of place or would have to know some particular historical fact about our church in order to participate are the points at which we should sit down and ask hard questions. What might it feel like to go to a Bible study group and not speak the dominant language? What could be good ways of dealing with that? At what point does it become a necessity for everyone to speak the same language? How can that point be moved or removed altogether?

The point is not to make services "seeker friendly" or to compromise to get people in the door. Instead, the point is to listen to others and put ourselves in their place to see where we have put unnecessary and unloving barriers in front of people being reached, taught, and discipled. Or to put it more simply, we need to ask where we are unintentionally pushing people away when God wants them to be drawn close.

Good Pain and Bad Pain

One reason why such changes can be difficult is that they can hurt. No one wants to hear that the Bible translation they love is incomprehensible for three-quarters of the people in the church. Few leaders look forward to hearing that their church has a racism problem or that people don't want to join the church after going to outreach activities for years. This kind of thing is painful.

But not all pain is the same. In early 2023, I went back to running after a long break due to becoming a dad for the fifth time. Before the break, I had reached the milestone of being able to run 8km (about 5 miles) and could conquer the worst hills my local area could throw at me. That made me think that a quick 3km run on my first week back would be easy.

That run was not easy. My breathing was labored. My feet felt like lead and within an hour of getting home, my legs felt like someone had repeatedly hit them. I was experiencing what the UK National Health Service poetically calls Delayed Onset Muscle Soreness (or DOMS) for short. There are lots of ways to ease DOMS, from light stretches to ice packs, but there is only one long-term cure if you have DOMS and not anything more serious.

That cure is to just get used to exercise.

You see, DOMS is a sign that your muscles have been pushed beyond what they are used to. It means that your muscles have suffered tiny tears, which can sometimes cause inflammation. But those tiny tears are how muscles get stronger. DOMS hurts and should be watched but it is actually a good kind of pain: the kind of pain that signals growth.

When managed well and worked through carefully, the pain of hearing what is and is not helpful can be the same for churches. It could be the micro tears, the productive tension that prompts a church to try something new, reach out in different ways, or even just to pay more attention to who comes into a meeting and make them feel at home. These tears and tension are signs of growth.

There is, of course, another kind of pain. I experienced that kind of pain when the church I attended in my teens and early twenties folded one Easter Sunday and I saw more than ten years of hard work and relationship building disappear. That pain meant finding a new church in which my wife and I had to start again. The pain of a church closing is much worse than the pain of walking through the discomfort of hearing how people are really experiencing the church.

This isn't some popularity exercise or even an experiment in trying to have people tell us how church should be done. No, listening to the experience of others is the tricky, beautiful, and loving journey of taking the time to slow down, listen, and reflect on someone else's experiences. And then it is the important work of walking through useful changes in behavior, attitudes, and even programs, to help people feel valued and loved and to experience God together with other believers. That, after all, is what the church has been since the book of Acts and what God is still calling the church to be today.

CHAPTER 16

Getting Help

This is where I begin to sign off. Here the emphasis moves from simply reading about multilingual church to doing it. This is where theory, research, and Bible reading become multilingual services, warmly welcoming churches, and I pray, communities changed as a result. It is also the beginning of reaching, teaching, and discipling everyone in your community, no matter which language they use.

I said previously that truly multilingual church is impossible without the power of God. Additionally, I believe that multilingual church is very difficult without expert help. While I am about to provide a list of useful resources, the greatest resources for multilingual churches, after the Bible, are simply other multilingual churches. There is no better way to learn than to be around others who are on the same path. Every other resource I will suggest will be useful, but none apart from the Bible will surpass the fellowship and encouragement of other like-minded churches and church leaders.

> There is no better way to learn than to be around others who are on the same path.

If you are looking for additional insights, here are lots of different resources, split into four categories.

Books

- **Building an International Church** by Pastor Mario Wahnschaffe. This book has provided some of the background material I referenced above and has significantly shaped my thinking. It offers levels of nitty-gritty detail that only an experienced pastor can and provides important real-life insights.
- **The High-Definition Leader: Building Multiethnic Churches in a Multiethnic World** by Derwin L. Grey. While he doesn't cover multilingual church, the author covers the biblical reasons for multiethnic church with a passion and power that is rare. He also carefully examines what this looks like in church and the attitudes needed to lead such churches.

- ***Multicultural Kingdom*** by Harvey Kwiyani. This book is unique in that it fuses tightly argued demographic analysis with a close reading of cultural and missional history and solid theology. It makes for uncomfortable reading at times, but it is the discomfort that produces growth.
- Mark DeYmaz and Harry Li have co-written a good number of books on multiethnic church, but I found ***Leading a Healthy Multi-Ethnic Church: Seven Common Challenges and How to Overcome Them*** and ***Ethnic Blends: Mixing Diversity into Your Local Church*** to be the most practical. The former also includes informative snippets from other multiethnic churches that may have parallels in other places.

Websites

- **ChurchInterpreting.com** offers free resources including articles and videos on the interpreting side of multilingual church.

Podcasts

- The Church Interpreting Podcast appears roughly every month, with new content for churches, interpreters, and preachers. Please note, the link is case sensitive. **https://bit.ly/ChurchInterpretingPodcast**

Organizations

- Intercultural Churches UK brings together UK churches who desire to become intercultural. They offer training days and webinars, and help to create fellowship between leaders of such churches. **https://icuk.network/about**

- Songs2Serve is the worship arm of Intercultural Churches UK, offering training and resources on multicultural worship. **https://songs2serve.eu**

- Here, Intercultural Ministries of the Assemblies of God in the USA offers important insight and resources. **https://intercultural.ag.org**

- The International Federation of Translators is the global federation of translation and interpreting associations. Using the link I provide here will take you to their list of members and direct you to your local association. They should be your first stop for professional support and advice on local training. https://en.fit-ift.org/members-directory
- CIUTI is the oldest organization bringing together universities offering training in translation and interpreting. Their list of members may include a university near you. Short courses offered by those universities can be an excellent way of gaining interpreting and translation skills. https://www.ciuti.org

The End Is the Beginning

It is my prayer that this book has inspired and equipped you and your church to go out and reach, teach, and disciple the multilingual community around you. If your church is not in a multilingual community, I pray that this book has provided a window into multilingual church and has given you a heart to support churches involved in this work. As the emphasis now moves from reading to doing, I would like to encourage all current and future multilingual churches that help is there. Feel free to contact me (jonathan@integritylanguages.co.uk) if you need any further support. And never forget that this is God's idea in the first place. Let's pray together.

> Father God, your Son reigns over every nation, tribe, and language. You began your church in a blaze of multilingual glory and you call us to walk by the power of your Spirit to reach the multilingual world around us. We cannot do this work on our own. We need the power of your Spirit, that same power that descended on your people in the upper room, the same power that gave Peter his vision, that same power that spoke to your church in Jerusalem. This is the power that raised Christ from the dead. You dwell in us by this same power. Father, bless everyone reading this book with the insight, wisdom, courage, and persistence to see your vision for multilingual, multicultural church become reality in their churches. Give them everything they need for the journey and may your kingdom come and your will be done on earth, as it is in heaven. In Jesus's mighty, powerful name we pray. Amen. So let it be.

AFTERWORD

I want to express my heartfelt gratitude to Jonathan, not just as a colleague and friend but as a distinguished language scholar who has broadened my horizons as a pastor and interpreter. Over the past few years, our paths have intertwined both personally and professionally, and it has been a rewarding journey.

Reflecting on my extensive experience as both a pastor and interpreter, I must confess that I've never come across a literary work quite like this one. It dives deeply into the profound impact of language on the church and ministry, and it does so in a remarkably unique and comprehensive manner.

For those pastors and leaders who have recently finished reading this book and are now pondering their next steps, allow me to offer a simple piece of advice: start at the beginning and keep it simple. Embrace the concepts presented here, with a special emphasis on those found in chapter 12—they have the potential to set you on an extraordinary growth path.

My dual role as a pastor and interpreter provides me with a unique perspective, one that enriches my understanding of the content within these pages. Coming from the multicultural city of Montreal, Quebec, Canada, I'm acutely aware of the aspirations shared by every kingdom-minded pastor: to witness the growth and expansion of their congregation, especially within the diverse tapestry of a multicultural urban setting.

The knowledge you've gained from this book is a key that can seamlessly integrate into your overarching vision and mission of saving souls in your city. I still vividly remember my first experience as an interpreter within a church setting where I witnessed the simultaneous interpretation of the French sermon into five or so languages. That pastor had already embraced the visionary concept of reaching souls from diverse cultural and linguistic backgrounds within our city.

During my extensive twenty-five-year journey as a Christian interpreter, I've had the privilege of interpreting for numerous remarkable men and women of God, conveying their awe-inspiring messages. Yet, my greatest joy is witnessing individuals embrace Jesus Christ as their Lord and Savior after hearing a message through an interpreter.

Pastors often gather their leadership teams around a conference room table to brainstorm ideas for church growth, plan events, extend guest invitations, and more. In light of the profound insights offered by this book, I firmly believe that divine inspiration may lead pastors and their leadership teams to consider the inclusion of interpreters as an integral facet of their future endeavors. The possibilities are boundless.

Mike Lemay
Pastor and interpreter, Montréal, Canada, 2024

ACKNOWLEDGMENTS

The very existence of this book is a testimony to the goodness of God, the patience of my family, and the space and time afforded by the National Library of Scotland, patient theologians and leaders, and the Acts2Terps church interpreter community. They say it takes a village to raise a child. In so many different ways, it feels like this book took a small town.

As I mentioned in the dedication, there is no way this book would even have been started without the encouragement, uplifting, and passion for God's kingdom displayed by my wife. I once flew to Germany to spend time with an English lady, and while there had my passion of multilingual church fanned into flame; it is no accident that that woman is now the person with whom I share my daily life. Helen, you are a wonderful wife, a superb mum, an incredible gift, and an answer to prayer. You are more gifted than you know and more special than you could possibly imagine.

My children (all six of them by the time you read this) deserve a big thank you for their patience with daddy making his laptop unavailable for videos and games, disappearing off to the National Library a few times, and talking about interpreting so much. Playing computer games and made-up games, reading and making up stories, discussing the Bible together, and even just playing in the park and sitting down for noisy family meals with you all are such a joy.

Mum, I know you pray for me every day. You have no idea how much those prayers mean to me. I also know you have been praying for this book. You have nurtured me in the faith since I was born. Our family walked through so much with you and dad as incredible examples. Thank you.

Dad, you would have loved to see this book. More than twenty years have passed since you died, and I still miss you. You and mum opened the house to anyone who came by—that decision led to this moment. Through that hospitality and encouraging all your children to go on mission trips, God birthed in me a passion for multilingual church. Thank you so much.

To my brother Paul, thank you for inspiring me by your passion for missions, your knowledge of Eastern Europe, and your continued hard work. May God bless the work of your hands.

To my sisters, Miriam and Evie, you two taught me so much. Miriam, your blogging, care for your family and persistence in incredibly trying circumstances are so powerful. Evie, your ability to thrive in academia, inspire students, and your readiness to travel crazy distances to spend time with people still astound me.

Harvey and Mike, you each knocked it out of the park with the Foreword and Afterword. I could not have imagined how eloquently each of you would write and the emotional impact it would have on me.

Acts2Terps crew, thank you so much for showing excitement about this project, helping to choose book covers, stirring my thinking, and sharing your stories. One day soon, I will write a book for church interpreters.

To Kirsty at Hope Counselling, you helped pull me out of a hole and set me back on track. It was meaningful that, in my last session, I got to tell you that I had signed the contract for this book. May God richly bless your powerful gift.

To everyone on the theres.life Mastodon instance: your responses to some of the key ideas from this book assured me that I was on the right track. Thank you for your support.

To Vivian, Brad, Mike, and everyone else (especially the copyediting team) at William Carey Publishing, thank you for taking a chance on a crazy Scot with an unusual book idea. I have never met such a friendly, approachable, and supportive team. The book you hold in your hands is a direct result of their patience and skill.

And last, but definitely not least, God, you have been with me through everything. I am very sure that I have left some deep grooves as I've been dragged along, rather than footprints, in the sand of my life sometimes. Multilingual church is your vision and it is an unbelievable privilege to play a tiny part in it. *Soli Deo Gloria.*

BIBLIOGRAPHY

Aldous, Ben, Idina Dunmore, and Mohan Seevaratnam. *Intercultural Church: Shared Learning from New Communities*. Grove Mission & Evangelism Series. Cambridge: Grove Books Limited, 2020.

Balci Tison, Alev. "The Interpreter's Involvement in a Translated Institution: A Case Study of Sermon Interpreting." PhD diss., Universitat Rovira i Virgili, 2016.

Braun, Sabine, and Judith Taylor. "Video-Mediated Interpreting: An Overview of Current Practice and Research." In *Videoconference and Remote Interpreting in Criminal Proceedings*, edited by Sabine Braun and Judith Taylor, 33–68. Antwerp: Intersential, 2012.

Carlson, Marvin. *Performance: A Critical Introduction*. London: Routledge, 1996.

Carter, Erik W., Michael Tuttle, Emilee Spann, Charis Ling, and Tiffany B. Jones. "Addressing Accessibility within the Church: Perspectives of People with Disabilities." *Journal of Religion and Health* 62, no. 4 (January 2022): 1–22. doi:10.1007/s10943-022-01508-6.

Clifford, Andrew. "Is Fidelity Ethical? The Social Role of the Healthcare Interpreter." *TTR: Traduction, Terminologie, Rédaction* 17, no. 2 (2004): 89–114.

Connor, Phillip, and Jens Manuel Krogstad. "5 Facts about the Global Somali Diaspora." *Pew Research Center*, June 1, 2016. https://www.pewresearch.org/short-reads/2016/06/01/5-facts-about-the-global-somali-diaspora/.

Darroch, Emma, and Raymond Dempsey. "Interpreters' Experiences of Transferential Dynamics, Vicarious Traumatisation, and Their Need for Support and Supervision: A Systematic Literature Review." *The European Journal of Counselling Psychology* 4, no. 2 (2016).

da Silva, Igor Antônio Lourenço da, Eliane Brito Soares, and Marileide Dias Esqueda. "Interpreting in a Religious Setting." *Tradução Em Revista* 2021, no. 30 (2018). https://doi.org/10.17771/PUCRio.TradRev.34553.

De Tan, Andrew Kai, Mansour Amini, and Kam-Fong Lee. "Challenges Faced by Non-Professional Interpreters in Interpreting Church Sermons in Malaysia." *International Online Journal of Language, Communication, and Humanities* 4, no. 1 (2021): 53–74.

DeYmaz, Mark, and Harry Li. *Leading a Healthy Multi-Ethnic Church: Seven Common Challenges and How to Overcome Them*. Grand Rapids, MI: Zondervan, 2013.

Diriker, Ebru. *De-/Re-Contextualizing Conference Interpreting: Interpreters in the Ivory Tower?* Vol. 53 of Benjamins Translation Library. Amsterdam: John Benjamins Publishing Company, 2004.

Downie, Jonathan. "Finding and Critiquing the Invisible Interpreter—A Response to Uldis Ozolins." *Interpreting* 19, no. 2 (2017): 260–70.

Downie, Jonathan "Stakeholder Expectations of Interpreters: A Multi-Site, Multi-Method Approach." PhD diss., Heriot-Watt University, 2016.

Downie, Jonathan, Alexander Drechsel, and Alexander Gansmeier. "Episode 17: Mental Health For Interpreters." *Troublesome Terps*, podcast. https://web.archive.org/web/20201031221144/https://www.troubleterps.com/17.

Downie, Jonathan, and Graham H. Turner. "Integrating Interpreting into Institutional Practice: Sign Language Interpreting in the Police and National Health Service in Scotland." *The Interpreter's Newsletter*, no. 13 (2021): 235–52. https://doi.org/10.13137/2421-714X/33273.

Edwards, Korie Little. "The Multiethnic Church Movement Hasn't Lived up to Its Promise." *Christianity Today*, February 16, 2021. https://www.christianitytoday.com/ct/2021/march/race-diversity-multiethnic-church-movement-promise.html.

Eraslan, Seyda. "International Knowledge Transfer in Turkey: The Consecutive Interpreter's Role in Context." PhD diss., Rovira i Virgili University, 2011.

"FAQ for Technicians | Interactio," 2023. https://www.interactio.io/faq/for-technicians#equipment-technicians.

Garces-Foley, Kathleen. *Crossing the Ethnic Divide: The Multiethnic Church on a Mission*. Oxford: Oxford University Press, 2007.

Gile, Daniel. *Basic Concepts and Models for Interpreter and Translator Training*, rev. ed. Amsterdam: John Benjamins Publishing Company, 2009.

Glickman, Michael. "The January 2018 School Census—What It Tells Us about Ethnicity and Language in Gateshead Schools." educationGateshead, May 2018. https://democracy.gateshead.gov.uk/documents/s16239/Item%2013%20Appendix%20Ethnicity%20and%20language%20from%20Jan%2018%20School%20Census.pdf.

Google Search Central. "Spam Policies for Google Web Search | Google Search Central | Documentation." Google for Developers, 2023. https://developers.google.com/search/docs/essentials/spam-policies.

Gray, Derwin L. *The High Definition Leader: Building Multiethnic Churches in a Multiethnic World*. Nashville, TN: Thomas Nelson, 2015.

Han, Huamei. "Social Inclusion through Multilingual Ideologies, Policies and Practices: A Case Study of a Minority Church." *International Journal of Bilingual Education and Bilingualism* 14, no. 4 (2011): 383–98.

Harkness, Nicholas. "Transducing a Sermon, Inducing Conversion: Billy Graham, Billy Kim, and the 1973 Crusade in Seoul." *Representations* 137, no. 1 (2017): 112–42.

Harris, Peter. "Parliament Hill Interpreter Hospitalized for 'Acoustic Shock.'" *Canada Today*, October 27, 2022.

Hayward, Victor, and Donald McGavran. "Without Crossing Barriers? One in Christ vs. Discipling Diverse Cultures." *Missiology: An International Review* 2, no. 2 (1974): 203–24. https://doi.org/10.1177/009182967400200207.

Hild, Adelina. "The Role and Self-Regulation of Non-Professional Interpreters in Religious Settings: The VIRS Project." In *Non-Professional Interpreting and Translation*, edited by Rachele Antonini, Letizia Cirillo, Linda Rossato, and Ira Torresi, 177–94. Amsterdam: John Benjamins Publishing Company, 2017.

Hokkanen, Sari. "Experiencing the Interpreter's Role: Emotions of Involvement and Detachment in Simultaneous Church Interpreting." *Translation Spaces* 6, no. 1 (2017): 62–78. https://doi.org/10.1075/ts.6.1.04hok.

Hokkanen, Sari. "Simultaneous Church Interpreting as Service." *The Translator: Studies in Intercultural Communication* 18, no. 2 (2012): 291–309. https://doi.org/10.1080/13556509.2012.10799512.

Hokkanen, Sari. "To Serve and to Experience: An Autoethnographic Study of Simultaneous Church Interpreting." PhD diss., Tampere University, 2016.

ID Community. "City of Perth: Languages Spoken at Home." City of Perth | Community Profile. Demographic Resources for the City of Perth, 2021. https://profile.id.com.au/perth/language.

Karlik, Jill. "Interpreter-Mediated Scriptures: Expectation and Performance." *Interpreting* 12, no. 2 (2010): 160–85. https://doi.org/10.1075/intp.12.2.03kar.

Karlik, Jill. "Translation and Performance: Interpreter Mediated Scriptures in Africa." In *Translating Scripture for Sound and Performance*, edited by James Maxey and Ernst R. Wendland. Eugene, OR: Cascade Books, 2012.

Kaufmann, Francine. "Contribution à l'histoire de l'interprétation consécutive: le metourguemane dans les synagogues de l'antiquité." *Meta: Journal Des Traducteurs/Translators' Journal* 50, no. 3 (2005): 972–86. https://doi.org/10.7202/011608ar.

Keijzer, Merel. "The Regression Hypothesis as a Framework for First Language Attrition." *Bilingualism: Language and Cognition* 13, no. 1 (January 2010): 9–18. https://doi.org/10.1017/S1366728909990356.

Kouega, Jean-Paul, and M. A. W. Ndzotom. "Multilingual Practices in Presbyterian Churches in Cameroon." *International Journal of Innovative Interdisciplinary Research* 1 (2011): 44–58.

Krihtova, Tatiana. "How to Enter the Church When the Door Is Closed. Language Policies in Christian Churches of Joensuu in the Context of a Migrant's Choice." *International Journal of Contemporary Economics and Administrative Sciences* 6 (2016): 41–51.

Kuruvilla, Abraham. *Text to Praxis: Hermeneutics and Homiletics in Dialogue*. London: T&T Clark, 2009.

Kwiyani, Harvey C. *Multicultural Kingdom: Ethnic Diversity, Mission and the Church*. London: SCM Press, 2020.

Lausanne Committee for World Evangelization. Lausanne Occasional Paper: "The Pasadena Consultation: Homogeneous Unit Principle." Pasadena, CA. 1978.

Lindemann, Verena. "Friedrich Schleiermacher's Lecture 'On the Different Methods of Translating' and the Notion of Authorship in Translation Studies." In *Rereading Schleiermacher: Translation, Cognition and Culture*, edited by Teresa Seruya and José Miranda Justo, 115–22. New Frontiers in Translation Studies. Berlin: Springer, 2016. https://doi.org/10.1007/978-3-662-47949-0_10.

Makha, Makhetsi, and Lehlohonolo Phafoli. "Distortion of Meaning in Consecutive Interpreting: Case Of Sermons in Selected Multicultural Churches in Maseru." *Journal of Applied Linguistics and Language Research* 6, no. 4 (2019): 152–63.

Marti, Gerardo. "Fluid Ethnicity and Ethnic Transcendence in Multiracial Churches." *Journal for the Scientific Study of Religion* 47, no. 1 (2008): 11–16.

Millard, Alan. "Reading and Writing In the Time of Jesus | Bible Interp." *The Bible and Interpretation*, January, 2000. https://bibleinterp.arizona.edu/articles/2000/Millard_Jesus.

Mouzourakis, Panayotis. "Remote Interpreting: A Technical Perspective on Recent Experiments." *Interpreting* 8, no. 1 (2006): 45–66.

Musyoka, Eunice Nthenya, and Peter N. Karanja. "Problems of Interpreting as a Means of Communication: A Study on Interpretation of Kamba to English Pentecostal Church Sermon in Machakos Town, Kenya." *International Journal of Humanities and Social Science* 4, no. 5 (March 2014): 196–207.

Napier, Jemina. "Interpreting Omissions: A New Perspective." *Interpreting* 6, no. 2 (2004): 117–42.

Napier, Jemina, Robert Skinner, and Graham H. Turner. "'It's Good for Them but Not so for Me': Inside the Sign Language Interpreting Call Centre." *Translation & Interpreting* 9, no. 2 (July 21, 2017): 1–23. https://doi.org/10.12807/t&i.v9i2.535.

National Records of Scotland. "Scotland's Census at a Glance: Languages." Scotland's Census, 2011. https://www.scotlandscensus.gov.uk/census-results/at-a-glance/languages/.

North Lanarkshire Council. "Wishaw Community Profile." Local Government Data Profile, May 2020. https://www.northlanarkshire.gov.uk/sites/default/files/2021-08/Abbreviated%20Wishaw%20Community%20Profile%20May%202020.pdf.

Office of National Statistics. "Language, England and Wales: Census 2021: Main Language, English Language Proficiency, and Household Language in England and Wales, Census 2021 Data." November 29, 2022. https://www.ons.gov.uk/peoplepopulationandcommunity/culturalidentity/language/bulletins/languageenglandandwales/census2021.

Office of National Statistics. "Religion, England and Wales: Census 2021: The religion of usual residents and household religious composition in England and Wales, Census 2021 Data." November 29, 2022. https://www.ons.gov.uk/peoplepopulationandcommunity/culturalidentity/religion/bulletins/religionenglandandwales/census2021.

Office of National Statistics. "Transcript of Census 2021 Topic Summaries Demography and Migration Video." *Census 2021*, November 2, 2022. https://www.ons.gov.uk/releases/demographyandmigrationcensus2021inenglandandwales.

Open Doors. "World Watch List 2023." https://www.opendoors.org/en-US/persecution/countries/.

Ortiz, Manuel. *One New People: Models for Developing a Multiethnic Church*. Downers Grove, IL: InterVarsity Press, 1996.

Patten, Malcolm. *Leading a Multicultural Church*. London: SPCK, 2016.

Peremota, Irina. "Church Interpreting in Evangelical Churches with Russian-Language Services." Master's thesis, University of Latvia, 2017.

Perez, Robert G. "Generating Trust in a Multiethnic 'Church of Christ/Iglesia de Cristo' in Santa Paula, California." PhD Thesis, Harding School of Theology, 2019. https://core.ac.uk/download/pdf/226779428.pdf.

Portes, Alejandro, and Lingxin Hao. "E Pluribus Unum: Bilingualism and Loss of Language in the Second Generation." *Sociology of Education* 71, no. 4 (1998): 269–94. https://doi.org/10.2307/2673171.

Portes, Alejandro, and Richard Schauffler. "Language and the Second Generation: Bilingualism Yesterday and Today." *International Migration Review* 28, no. 4 (December 1, 1994): 640–61. https://doi.org/10.1177/019791839402800402.

Rayman, Jennifer. "Visions of Equality: Translating Power in a Deaf Sermonette." *The Sign Language Translator and Interpreter* 1, no. 1 (2007): 73–114.

Reynolds, Christopher. "Parliamentary Hearings over Zoom an Ongoing Headache for Interpreters." *CBC News*, January 20, 2021. https://www.cbc.ca/news/politics/parliamentary-translators-survey-1.5879907.

Reynolds, Susan B., and Andrew D. Reynolds. "The Integration of Hispanic Parishioners in US Catholic Parishes with Hispanic Ministry: Results from a National Survey." *Journal of Prevention & Intervention in the Community* 46, no. 4 (October 2, 2018): 355–71. https://doi.org/10.1080/10852352.2018.1507496.

Riggio, Allison J. "MAP: The Languages We Speak Behind Closed Doors." *Crain's Chicago Business*. Audio, November 2, 2013. https://www.chicagobusiness.com/article/20131102/ISSUE01/131029782/what-languages-does-chicago-speak-at-home.

Starks, Brian, and Gary J. Adler. "What Veteran Parishes Can Teach Us: How Long-Serving Spanish-Language Ministries Successfully Integrate Latinos within the Parish." *Journal of Prevention & Intervention in the Community* 46, no. 4 (October 2, 2018): 340–54. https://doi.org/10.1080/10852352.2018.1507495.

Scazzero, Peter. *Emotionally Healthy Spirituality: It's Impossible to Be Spiritually Mature, While Remaining Emotionally Immature*. Grand Rapids, MI: Zondervan, 2017.

Scott, Graham R., and Eleonora L. Scott. "Heart-Language Worship in Multilingual Contexts." *Crucible* 4, no. 1 (2012).

Sherwood, Harriet. "British Public Turn to Prayer as One in Four Tune in to Religious Services." *The Observer*, May 3, 2020, sec. World News. https://www.theguardian.com/world/2020/may/03/british-public-turn-to-prayer-as-one-in-four-tune-in-to-religious-services.

Starks, Brian, and Gary J. Adler. "What Veteran Parishes Can Teach Us: How Long-Serving Spanish-Language Ministries Successfully Integrate Latinos within the Parish." *Journal of Prevention & Intervention in the Community* 46, no. 4 (2 October 2018): 340–54. https://doi.org/10.1080/10852352.2018.1507495.

Tekgül, Duygu. "Faith-Related Interpreting as Emotional Labour: A Case Study at a Protestant Armenian Church in Istanbul." *Perspectives* 28, no. 1 (2020): 43–57. https://doi.org/10.1080/0907676X.2019.1641527.

Vigouroux, C. B. "Double-Mouthed Discourse: Interpreting, Framing, and Participant Roles." *Journal of Sociolinguistics* 14, no. 3 (2010): 341–69. https://doi.org/10.1111/j.1467-9841.2010.00448.x.

W3Techs. "Usage Statistics and Market Share of Content Languages for Websites, July 2023." Usage statistics of content languages for websites, July 2023. https://w3techs.com/technologies/overview/content_language.

Wahnschaffe, Mario. *Building an International Church*. Self-published, Amazon Digital Services, 2017. Kindle.

Wesley, John. *The Journal of the Reverend John Wesley: Sometime Fellow of Lincoln College, Oxford*. J. Emory and B. Waugh. London, 1832.

visit us at missionbooks.org

A Better Country: Embracing the Refugees in Our Midst (Second Edition)

Cindy M. Wu

A Better Country aims to help Christians think theologically and practically about the ongoing and changing refugee needs. This workbook is divided into six lessons followed by a personal action plan as your application. This resource balances information and reflection that will stimulate excellent group discussions and individual study.

People Disrupted: Doing Mission Responsibly among Refugees and Migrants

Jinbong Kim, Dwight P. Baker, Jonathan J. Bonk, J. Nelson Jennings, Jae Hoon Lee, Editors

This volume is the outcome of the multinational case studies and responses presented at the Korean Global Mission Leadership Forum consultation held in Sokcho, Korea, in 2017. The studies presented deal with significant issues in Christian mission, such as North Korean migrants, the sufferings of Iraqis fleeing from war, African refugees, Syrian refugees in Lebanon, overseas Filipino workers, and other refugee cases.

Language Learning in Ministry: Preparing for Cross-Cultural Language Acquisition

Jan Edwards Dormer

This book is essential for learning a new language or providing guidance for those headed into a new language context. With chapters on both formal and informal language learning to guide the selection of language schools, programs, and methodologies, this book walks you through the options, opportunities, and challenges ahead.

www.ingramcontent.com/pod-product-compliance
Lightning Source LLC
Chambersburg PA
CBHW052141070526
44585CB00017B/1929